TYNEHAM

Lilian Bond was born in 1887. Her father inherited the manor of Tyneham in 1898 and it was there that she spent her childhood and adolescence. *Tyneham – A Lost Heritage* is her account of those years. Although her only book, it quickly won her a host of admirers when it was first published in 1956 and is now widely regarded as a Dorset classic. Following her marriage to Ivo Bond in 1914 she moved to Weybridge and Windsor, only returning to Dorset after her husband's retirement in 1949. By then Tyneham had been evacuated, and *Tyneham* was written in response to the many requests that she provide a permanent record of its people and way of life. Lilian Bond died in 1980.

TYNEHAM

A Lost Heritage

LILIAN BOND

THE DOVECOTE PRESS

First published in 1956
This edition first published in 1984 by The Dovecote Press Ltd
Stanbridge, Wimborne, Dorset

ISBN 0 946159 18 1

© The Friary Press Ltd 1984
Printed and bound in Great Britain by
Biddles Ltd, Guildford, Surrey

FOREWORD

PURBECK is a kind of inner shrine of coastal England—perhaps its oldest inhabited corner, for long one of its most solitary, and still, despite the continuing depredations of war and the War Department, one of its most beautiful. Along its southern shore lie three beautiful manor-houses, Encombe, Smedmore and, loveliest of all, Tyneham. Encombe, though shorn for England's sake of most of the noble trees that gave its deep and secret dell the name of Golden Valley, is still occupied by the family that built it. Smedmore, ravaged and made desolate by Army occupation, has now been restored to its former beauty—a long labour of love in which the present writer bore some part—but has now, alas, to undergo a further restoration from the less showy but even more devastating ravages of death-watch beetle. The hardest fate of all has befallen Tyneham which, with its exquisite village and Worbarrow Bay—surely the loveliest in England—was taken over during the War for training the American and British Armies for their great mission on D-day, but then, after the War, despite a solemn assurance by the requisitioning Government, by a lamentable breach of faith retained as part of a Gunnery Range. The villagers have never been allowed to return to their homes; the Bond family—Tyneham's owners and occupiers for hundreds of happy creative years—have been made exiles from it for ever; the beautiful Elizabethan manor-house, among its walled gardens, deep, cool wells and embowering woods, has been left—the prey of ricochetting shells—to rot and decay; and the notice-board, which during the War years recorded the Nation's promise to restore to those whose forbears had made them the homes in which they had been born, has been removed by Authority.

Yet man's spirit has a way in the end of triumphing over physical defeat and

"John Barleycorn got up again
And sore surprised them all"

Mrs. Bond, who for so long lived in this dear, much-loved place, has recreated its life in time out of time and given for generations that will never have known it a portrait of the kind of life that good, contented and industrious men and women lived there throughout the centuries that made England. When mankind, now on the march, repitches its tents, it may help to remind it of how an enduring home can be made.

ARTHUR BRYANT.

October, 1956

INTRODUCTION

The Bond family has been prominent in Dorset, particularly in Purbeck, for several centuries and its members have filled a variety of undemanding public and private posts throughout this time – squires, parsons, lawyers, Army officers, Mayors, Justices of the Peace and Members of Parliament – but few, if any, have possessed the many talents and versatility of Lilian Bond, the author of this book.

Lilian May Garneys Bond was born on March 20th, 1887. Her parents, William Henry Bond and his wife, Mary Caroline, second daughter of Sir Harry Meysey Thompson, Bart. of Kirkby Hall, Yorkshire, were then living at Fryern Court, near Fordingbridge. Her father inherited the manor of Tyneham in 1898 and Tyneham House became her beloved home until her marriage in 1914. Here she spent the most impressionable years of her life observing with an artist's keen eye the beauties of sea, sky, coast and valley, and the ebb and flow of the tides and seasons.

Her eldest brother, Algernon, severely wounded at the Siege of Ladysmith, died prematurely and she was fortunate to be able to turn to her other brother Ralph, her senior by seven years, to draw upon his already extensive knowledge of both natural and local history. She and her sisters were educated entirely at home by a Russian governess, Miss Sokolova, who was obviously an inspired teacher and who is well described in this book. She clearly detected, awakened and encouraged the latent talents of her pupils and laid the foundations for Lilian's later reading and study.

On January 18th, 1914, Lilian was married at Tyneham to Herbert Ivo de Kenton Bond, seventh surviving son of Nathaniel Bond of another Purbeck country house, Creech Grange, and Lady Selina Jane, daughter of the second Earl of Eldon. For the next thirty-five years they lived at Weybridge and Windsor until on Ivo's retirement they returned to Dorset, joining her younger sister Margot in 1949. From then on they played a full part in Dorset life, particularly in the activities of the County Museum and its controlling body, the Dorset Natural History and Archaeological Society. For her outstanding contribution to the Society Lilian was elected, in 1964, the first lady member of the Council and in 1967 was made a Vice President.

Although it is true that Lilian made quite frequent visits to Tyneham between 1914 and the outbreak of the Second World War, and that she was always warmly welcomed there by her parents and latterly by her brother Ralph, she may perhaps have felt herself to some extent an 'exile' since her marriage. This may be the reason why the memories recalled in this book seem to possess the crystalline clarity of childhood's total recall, rather than the blurred result of a lifetime's knowledge of Tyneham and its way of life. Certainly she saw her early years at Tyneham as a 'Golden Age' and the glow of her memory reflects this view.

The compulsory wartime evacuation of Tyneham in 1943, the calculated neglect and vandalism to which her old home was subsequently subjected, and the Government's broken promise to return Tyneham to her brother Ralph after the war, hurt her dreadfully. She never became reconciled to this loss and, when public access to the Valley eventually became possible, she steadfastly refused to visit it and see it in its decline, preferring to retain intact those early radiant memories which she so luminously discloses in this book.

In addition to natural and local history, her interests included the Dorset dialect, genealogy, family history – upon which she was an expert – theology and hagiology. She was a gifted and versatile actress performing in semi-professional productions for charity when living in Weybridge and earlier in a more amateur fashion in pantomimes, which she wrote herself and were produced in Tyneham Farm Barn. The pen and ink sketches with which she illustrated her letters and adorned birthday cards and greetings were of a high standard and her occasional verses were distinguished by delicacy of thought and clarity of expression. She was a truly remarkable correspondent: her letters – replies always by return of post – were masterpieces of entertainment, wit, description and comment. She had the ability to carry out, by post, a leisurely and enjoyable conversation with those who wrote to her which the age of the telephone has sadly curtailed. She wrote a daily letter to her mother for thirty-five years and every Christmas wrote a special letter to several hundred friends and relations until she was well into her nineties – quite apart from her normal voluminous daily correspondence.

No account of her life would be complete without mention of her profound belief in the Christian faith and of her generous, charitable and Christian life. Despite occasional ill-health, she lived for ninety-three years, dying at Branksome, Poole, on August 12th, 1980.

Undoubtedly this book is her greatest literary legacy. It was first published in 1956 and as a record of Purbeck life it cannot be bettered. The tragic events to befall Tyneham add to its importance, transforming it from an evocative record of a vanished way of life into a portrait of Tyneham and its world that is irreplaceable. She was justifiably proud of it and would have been delighted by the appearance of this new edition.

MAJOR-GENERAL H. M. G. BOND, JP, DL

CONTENTS

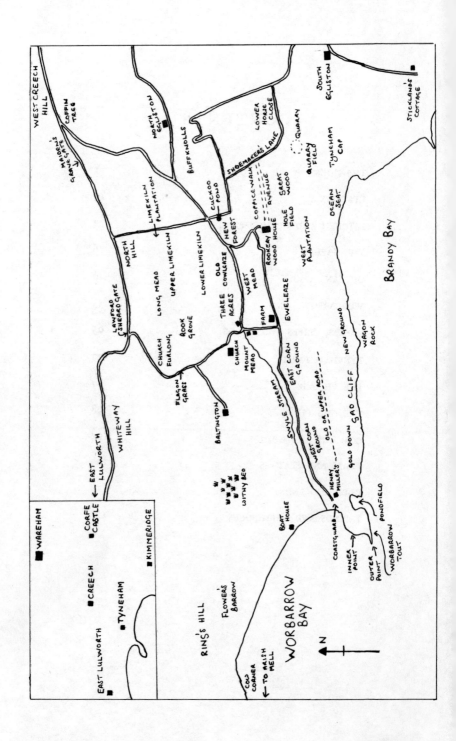

INTRODUCTORY NOTE

SO many friends have asked me for a picture of a vanished Tyneham and its people that their requests may possibly excuse the addition of yet one more book of country memories to the long list of those already in existence.

The Tyneham that we knew has gone for ever and it appears deplorable to those who cared for it that so much loveliness should pass into oblivion, leaving no record for the coming generations. It has been said that "remembrance is as vital to nations as to men" and somewhere Hilaire Belloc has remarked that "the corner of a corner of England is infinite and can never be exhausted". But, owing to the action of the War Department, there is no Tyneham dweller left to hand on the traditions of the valley, and the few initiates among the banished who still treasure them will soon have passed away.

There must be many thousands who have visited the hidden sanctuary and found themselves compelled to return to it over and over again, drawn by its irresistible charm.

On numberless occasions, in places far from Purbeck, I have met chance acquaintances who, when the talk has turned on Dorset, spoke of one corner of it which they had "discovered", a corner so remote that they thought it hardly likely I should know its name. The spot they knew and loved was, almost without exception, Tyneham.

To these and other friends of Tyneham, in all parts of the world, this very imperfect record of a place and way of life now disappeared is offered, without apology for its total lack of literary merit. Its subject will, I hope, excuse to them its want of style and form and method of selection. I only ask them to regard it as an honest attempt to describe a life-time's memories of a well-loved home.

TYNEHAM

I shall not cross the sleeping hill
  Nor take the homeward road again,
The whispering woods, the hidden vale,
  The soft winds call to me in vain.

I shall not see your blinded face,
  Dear house now crumbling slow to dust,
I will not gaze upon your death
  Who gave me life to hold in trust.

Your kindly hearthstone has grown cold,
  Yet silently your faith you keep
(Mute victim of the strife of men)
  With generations long asleep.

They say your beauty haunts you still,
  Wrought out through all the patient years,
And breathes an immemorial peace
  Transcending mortal hopes and fears.

The peace of God, dispensed to men
  With hearts to service consecrate
In loyal thraldom to the land
  And courtesy to small and great.

So, dying, in your old grey stones
  Unmeasured memories remain,
The long-lost silence of the world,
  The grace that will not come again.

CHAPTER I

The House

TO those who never visited the valley I cannot hope to convey its atmosphere and spirit which were unique and gave to Tyneham its peculiar fascination.

Descriptions of the ancient house and the surrounding country may indeed bring back to those who loved them something of their quiet, compelling charm, but its quality is inexpressible in words and that elusive quality was the essential Tyneham.

How real it was, even to casual visitors and sightseers, is proved by the assurances of many upon whom it left a deep impression. They felt that it resembled nothing that they had experienced before, a sense of peaceful continuity hitherto undreamed of.

The valley was remote, so far from busy roads and railway that no sound of traffic ever disturbed its quiet, but many other places as remote and silent are without the quality of Tyneham's peacefulness, a quietude unstirred by surface happenings, having its roots in centuries of loving care and calm, unhurried occupation.

It seemed as if Tyneham's deep serenity had left an imprint on the children it had bred and, in its turn, had taken the impression of their peaceful, ordered lives, laying up stores of ever deepening tranquility to bless successive generations.

It took me many years to appreciate this but, even as a child, I never left the place without reluctance and never failed to sense the keen enchantment of return to something dimly realised as part of my own self and of whose continuing life I formed a part.

The spell of Tyneham gave me a criterion, and other places which might rival and surpass its outward beauty failed to survive the test of being compared with it for inward peace. No member of the family, to my knowledge, ever left Tyneham without regret or severed his connection with the ancient home without necessity. There was an old tradition that no Bond of Grange could live long out of sight of Creech Barrow and certainly a Tyneham Bond must touch his native soil, from time to time, Antæos-wise, in order to survive in full content.

When we came home from exile in the outside world the first real breath of Tyneham met us as we left Wood Lane for the open backbone of the Purbeck range. All through the hour's drive (for I am thinking now of the horse-drawn journeys back from Wareham station before 1926) the unbroken line of the hills had closed the distant view, hiding

I

the Tyneham valley and the sea. Those leisurely drives enhanced the pleasures of anticipation, giving us time to savour all the loved, well-known enchantments of the way. During the long, slow climb from Stoborough to Grange the wooded barrier seemed to grow in height until we reached the spot at the top of the park at Grange where passengers turned out to mount the hill on foot, and then the hanging woods rose steeply, close above our heads. Pulling an empty carriage up the merciless incline was strain enough for tired horses, a strain increased when snow or ice lay on the sharper pitches of the road. So, wet or fine, by day or night, in every season of the year, both young and old reduced the load by walking up the hill. We took it as a matter of course, as we took the opening of the gates which barred the roads, and were contented with the slowness of our progress.

Until the years which followed the First World War eleven gates still marked the two mile stretch of road between Tyneham and Steeple Church and there were eight to be negotiated on the Wareham road between the top of "Bond Street", at Grange Gate, and the House at Tyneham. A ride along the hills to Chapman's Pool involved the opening of seventy.

When cars grew common a demand arose for roadside fencing to eliminate the gates and minimise the risk of accidents with cattle, and so the ugly barriers arrived to stay and, for the walker, rider, child and dog the pleasure and the safety of the open road was done away.

The advent of the petrol engine robbed us of another pleasure of the earlier days for, in the course of many climbs on foot through Grange Great Wood, we came to know and enjoy each wayside detail of the long ascent. Broomrape and toothwort, delicate wood melick grass and barren strawberry, spindle, dewberry and burnet rose, wood sorrel, broad-leaved helleborine and many rarer flowers grew in the moss-clothed banks beside the road. Their cool, sweet, earthy scents accompanied the climber to the crest of the hill. Then, as from the sudden opening of an outer door, a different air, the clean salt breath of the sea and the Tyneham valley, healing, reviving and exhilarating, met and refreshed the traveller. That air was unlike any other. The downs at Swanage had a fragrance which came somewhere near it but breezes from the neighbouring places on the coast, outside Purbeck—Ringstead, Osmington or Weymouth—resembled it not at all. What was the essence of that delectable air, peculiar to the valley at all seasons of the year? The scents of beans in flower, of sea-weed, haygrass, clover, burning couch, of storm-bruised leaves and new-turned earth, of gorse in blossom, sun-dried grass and many other ingredients came and departed with the changing year, but the underlying redolence of Tyneham remained the same throughout the months, familiar to the valley dweller as the basic smell of smoke and petrol is to the townsman.

It did, in fact, intensify the scent of Tyneham flowers, as Tyneham soil or air intensified the brilliance of their colours. How often have I hopefully set plants or seeds from Tyneham in my urban garden, only to meet with disappointment when the poor, pale travesties of their Purbeck kinsfolk came into flower.

The traveller along the ridge as far as Steeple Cross looked out to the north across the dark expanse of Hardy's Egdon Heath, from the creeks and islets of Poole Harbour to the monument on Blagdon and past the highlands of North Dorset to where Alfred's Tower stands sentinel at the meeting place of Dorset, Somerset and Wiltshire. The view of this great sweep of open country has become well known and popular and it is beautiful in its changing aspects at each season of the year.

But we, returning home, had eyes for the valley only, the valley, sea and landlocked, with its unsymmetric pattern of green fields inlaid with grey stone walls and quick-set hedges, its hanging woods and belts and coppices, its little groups of trees encircling cottages and farms, each neatly fitting piece of the intricate design familiar to us as the patterns of the carpets in our rooms.

Eastwards the double line of hills swept back in parallel curves to Corfe, the southern ridge between valley and sea crowned five miles away by the tower of Street's tall church at Kingston. A dip in the ridge showed Smedmore's grey façade clear cut against shadowy woods and, in the nearer valley, the sturdy tower of Steeple Church lay girdled by its trees.

When I was young the downland still possessed a thriving populace of sheep and all day long the sheep bells chimed and echoed to and fro between the hills.

The House was out of sight from the Wareham road, lying beyond a grassy ridge of the valley floor and sheltered by its plantings, but the Great Wood and the West Plantation close behind the House were plain to view as they climbed the hillside almost to the jagged and tilted edge of Gadcliff. Not until travellers were halfway down the Cowleaze Knap, with only a couple of hundred yards to go, did a glimpse of the walls and chimneys show between the trees. And then at last the vista of the 'Gap' was opened up and the mullioned windows of the tall north gable came into sight.

My memories of Tyneham cover many years and sometimes as I write I am a child again, sometimes grown up and coming back for longer or shorter periods in my parents' house, but always the return to Tyneham, even on a visit, was "coming home".

The child whose turn it was to open the last gate and shut it carefully once more against the cattle on the Knap, sped down the grassy slope between the trees to reach the House before the carriage could complete its longer circuit. In summer-time my father would be sitting out by the garden porch, watching for our arrival, and would come to the terrace steps to greet us with an escort of ecstatic dogs. My mother would leave her gardening to join in the welcome.

In winter the first to reach the 'new' north porch would set the great front-doorbell clanging through the house, then run three steps at a time up the flight of bare stone stairs to the warm and welcoming Oak Hall. Tea would be ready for us on the gate-legged table in the lamplight and a hot fire crackling in the "tortoise" stove.

The Oak Hall was a square room facing east with an entrance from the terrace. Its window overlooked the lawn and the long grassed slope of the avenue to where, a quarter of a mile away, it met the sky. In earlier days the carriage drive had circled round the lawn and reached the terrace entrance from the south. In 1862 my great-uncle, the Reverend John Bond, built the new north porch and entrance hall, bringing the drive to this new door from the foot of the slope.

At a yet earlier time a courtyard with a gatehouse filled the space between the House and avenue and still, in hot, dry seasons, outlines of vanished walls could be discerned in the turf of the lawn, but there is no record of the date when the courtyard disappeared. My father believed that the Chinese Chippendale gates into the Rookery Wood and Coppice Walk were copied from the courtyard entrances. The Oak Hall owed its name to its polished floorboards, not to the panelling, of later date than that in the rest of the house and of oak-grained pine. The panels were topped by coats of arms all round the room, from the arms of Lutton to my father's coat impaled with the cinquefoils and falcons of the Meysey-Thompsons.

The Oak Hall is associated in my mind with my great-uncle John. He was well into his nineties when I first made friends with him, and hearing and sight were fast forsaking him but mind and wit and outlook were still young and fresh. My memory holds a clear-cut picture of his tall, slight figure in old-fashioned clerical black, with shirt and socks and bow tie all of snowy white, emerging from the library to say a kind, affectionate word to the child in the hall. His face was beautiful, with finely sculptured bones and ivory complexion. But what endeared him to me was his gentle voice and manner, matching the kindness of his blue-grey eyes and putting the shyest child immediately at ease. He must have been exceedingly attractive in his younger days and doubtless found it difficult to escape the attentions of the ladies in his Somerset congregation. He treasured one anonymous declaration in which the writer catalogued her many attractions and begged him to look out for her in a certain pew on the following Sunday. He took good care to avert his eyes from that pew throughout the sermon.

As I remember him he was too feeble to do more than potter round the garden, taking keen interest in the bird and insect life as well as in the trees and flowering shrubs of his own planting. He liked to show me where the nuthatches had wedged the hazel nuts into the crevices of the elm bark, which held them as in a vice for cracking purposes. I have often wished I had been old enough to profit more by his extensive knowledge of wild life. I wish, too, that I might have listened to his reminiscences, for he had a retentive memory which took him back to the nineteenth century's very early years. His youth was lived before the age of railways, matches, electricity and many other inventions taken by the later generations as a matter of course and considered by them to be necessities of life. During his long incumbency of Weston, close to Bath (he was its parish priest for fifty-five years) his younger brother Tom, the antiquarian, kept house at Tyneham, at first with his two sisters, afterwards alone, and managed the estates. Tom was the delicate youngest of the family of six but outlived them all with the exception of his brother John. It was, I think, on Uncle Tom's account that a house was bought—or built?—at Bournemouth for long sojourns in the last few winters of his life. When young the brothers used to ride along the coast to the little group of fishermen's houses and the "Tregonwell Arms", which formed the whole of Bournemouth at that date, crossing the ferry at Sandbanks with their horses. Great-uncle John was nearly ninety-eight when he slipped away as quietly and unobtrusively as he had lived, leaving a memory of great goodness and fidelity.

The hall and drawing room had lost their mullioned windows in the reign of my great-grandmother, a Biggs of Stockton in the Wylye Valley. Coming to Tyneham early in the nineteenth century she, like so many others of her time, disliked "old-fashioned windows", of which she had had enough in her girlhood's home at Stockton. And so the ground floor mullions of the eastern front gave way to light-framed sashes. Her youngest son, great-uncle Tom, remembered the original windows and, after many years, set an exact facsimile of them in the north wall of the library. The old stone traceries were dumped out in the Stable Plot above the cowhouse and there they remained, moss-grown and sunk into the ground when the house was disinhabited. There was recurring talk of having them replaced but it never came to anything, the family being of a mind that the harm was done and that the sashes let in far more air and light than their ancient predecessors could have done. Time had toned down the existing stonework to the colour of the walls and replacement of the mullions must have left unsightly scars for many years.

The library to the north of the hall was a peaceful room, well-lined with bookcases from floor to ceiling, pervaded with that mellow scent of ancient bindings able to evoke deep-buried memories even when met with in improbable settings. The old editions of the classics did not tempt us overmuch, but the works on natural history were an abiding joy, Buffon, Bewick, Yarrell, Sowerby, Morris, Curtis and the like, the calf-bound volumes arrayed in orderly rows and occupying many shelves, for Uncle John was deeply interested in many provinces of natural science. My father sold a waggon-load of books, two tons of them, to Sotheby, but their departure seemed to make no difference to the crowding of the shelves.

The drawing-room across the hall was a delectable place, with two long windows looking east and one to the south, so shielded by the thickness of its Purbeck ashlar walls that no extreme of outside temperature could affect its comfort. A wide steel grate in the William and

5

Mary fireplace shed a roasting heat when heaped with logs on winter nights. We used to count the minutes to the end of lessons as we sat in the draughty schoolroom after tea and, when the clock struck six, stampeded down the stairs to the grateful comfort of the drawing-room hearth. My mother loved to have us with her there and often read aloud to us while we drew or knitted or sewed according to out tastes.

Between the two east windows hung a tall French mirror over the cupboard which for generations had been used for storing indoor games. It housed a good variety of favourites of many different periods:—old ivory chessmen exquisitely carved, a box of fish-shaped counters cut from mother-of-pearl, a solitaire board rubbed bright by years of handling, the old original "Happy Families" and "Animal Lotto", draughts, halma, reversi and backgammon boards, a set of delicate ivory spillikins, a box of letters used for spelling games, and many other carefully cherished games and toys which had been handed on from one generation to another. The lowest shelf of the cupboard held our picture books, amongst them the original Caldecotts and "Struwelpeter", "The Horkey Night", "The Funny Foxes" and "Hookey-beak The Raven" together with a collection of small books of moral verse and tales from Early Victorian times. Here, too, were kept our Sunday cut-out puzzles, forerunners of the jig-saw family, with gaily coloured Bible pictures cut in large and easy shapes. What was the game played on a chequer-board with fascinating "men" of heavy coloured glass, shaped like the paperweights now all the rage, in amber, emerald green, deep ruby red and milky white? I cannot now recall the rules or object of the game, but the feel of the smooth glass drops is in my fingers still.

The drawing-room walls were wainscoted with well proportioned panels, painted in soft, warm biscuit shade and outlined in dull gold, the perfect background for my great-aunt Mary's sea and landscapes. The paintings were exactly suited to the room besides possessing merit in themselves, for the artist's talent was considerably greater than the average amateur's. Here, as in all the other rooms, the furniture was representative of many dates and periods, a nightmare to the purist but entirely satisfactory to such as liked a house to be a family home instead of a collection. I still remember Detmar Blow's delight on his first introduction to the contents of the house. He had so often been required to furnish country houses "to a period", with all the landmarks of successive generations' tastes obliterated, that he hailed with relief the evidence, at Tyneham, of centuries of domestic history. He begged that nothing might be changed to satisfy a more pedantic or sophisticated taste, and held, with E. M. Almedingen that

"Things owned in pride and love
Still keep the touch of fingers lost in dust,
Things once looked upon enclose the secrets
Of eyes which see no more."

6

The proofs of continuity appealed to him as no artistic arrangement by a single mind and hand could ever do.

In one east window stood a little work table of the Regency period with a semi-circular drawer fronted with pleated sage-green silk, and, by the companion window, the great china jar of pot-pourri, never replenished within living memory but still giving out the ghost of a delicate fragrance, as every child of the house discovered for itself as soon as it was tall and strong enough to lift the heavy cover by its gilded knob.

On one side of the hearth a graceful cabinet of marqueterie contained an array of fans and china seen through glass-paned doors, and a specimen table under the south window held a quantity of modest treasures added to by each successive generation. Here were the family miniatures, amongst them one of Sir William Dutton Colt in a lovely oval setting of rose diamonds. Sir William was Prince Rupert's Master of the Horse and Envoy to the Courts of Brunswick, Dresden, Celle and Hanover. He saved Dutch William's life by his discovery and frustration of a plot to assassinate the King. His daughter married as her second husband Denis Bond of Grange and her child by a former marriage, Mary Dummer, afterwards became the wife of Denis' nephew John, of Tyneham and of Grange, the "common ancestor" of my husband and myself. The miniature of Sir William is, so far as I know, the only portrait of him in existence. When W. H. Wilkins was staying at Lulworth Castle, engaged in gathering material for his work "The Love of an Uncrowned Queen", he visited Tyneham and was shown the miniature, in which he showed much interest, having searched in vain through public and private galleries for a portrait of the Envoy.

Another charming miniature was that of my great-great-grand-father, the aforesaid John, a son of Tyneham who inherited Grange, shown as a young man in a powdered tie-wig, flower-embroidered satin waistcoat and velvet coat of an exquisite shade of hyacinth blue. It was he who made the Little Wood at Grange, planting the barren heathland with long avenues of Scots and silver firs and laying out the Long Canal and lower ponds which were to give such lasting pleasure to succeeding generations. He represented Corfe in Parliament for over thirty years and was beloved by friends and neighbours in every walk of life. The miniature portrays a man of sensibility and cheerful spirit, an impression not belied by the sitter's later life. He and his Mary must have been a lovable pair, to judge by their affectionate correspondence while he was away at Westminster and she was left in charge at Grange. Their happy married life flowed on for thirty-five years and, when it ended with his death at the age of sixty-six in 1784, she quickly followed him. John's personality impressed me when I was a child and I still consider him the perfect type of a Christian Englishman, remarkable in all his various relationships, as son and husband, father, brother, neighbour, squire and public servant. In spite of all his

7

manifold activities he was a lover of books and diligent reader, proficient in law and a notable classical scholar.

The miniature portraits of John and Mary's children—six, of whom four were boys—were set together in one case. The boys were: the second John of Grange, Nathaniel of East Holme, Thomas of Egliston and Wool Bridge, and William, my great-grandfather, of Tyneham. Their eldest sister, Margaret, became the wife of the Rev. John Methuen Rogers of Berkeley House in Somerset and Mary, the younger, married Nicholas Corsellis of Wivenhoe in Essex. Her marriage ended in disaster almost as soon as it had begun. The story went that as the couple drove away from church on their wedding day, Corsellis broke it to the bride that he had a natural daughter living in his home and Mary, without more ado, jumped out of the carriage to go back to her father's house for good. Her Nicholas seems to have been an eccentric man by all accounts and his doings are still a legend in the neighbourhood of Wivenhoe, where tales of his wild riding through the night and other strange proceedings linger on, so Mary may have had an excuse for her behaviour. She seems to have transferred her interests and affections to a horde of cherished cage-birds and scattered about the house at Tyneham there were many mahogany tables, large and small, specially made with "galleries" to fit the cages. A few of the old Corsellis spoons—a wedding gift no doubt—of elegant design and worn to paper thinness, survived into our times. According to a family tradition "Aunt Corsellis" fell asleep one evening after dinner, to the unconcealed amusement of her brothers who were in the room. She woke to find them laughing and was so incensed that, true to her old impetuosity, she cut the offending brothers out of her will.

The specimen table held many odds and ends of family possessions, of value through their known or guessed associations:—some beautiful old watches, one globe-shaped in a shagreen case; an etui, also in shagreen, fitted with implements for needlework; another in ivory; fobs; seals; innumerable mourning-rings bearing dates, initials, tiny plaits of the departed's hair, little intaglio pictures of broken columns, urns, weeping willows and drooping female figures; pounce, snuff and comfit-boxes; vinaigrettes; the box of chocolate received by my elder brother, in common with all the other combatants in the South African campaign, from Queen Victoria, and many other relics of the past.

The whole room had an atmosphere of spiritual as well as of physical comfort and well-being, as if the gentle presences of vanished occupants informed it still. What Phyllis Legh has said of the drawing-room at Lyme was true of its humbler counterpart at Tyneham:—"It seemed to breathe peace, to murmur of happiness, a happiness of lives spent in love and charity, and leisure which had not been abused and humility whose pride was service . . . . Beautiful, gentle old world, beautiful, sweet and gentle, loved and loving old home".

Facing the stairway from the entrance hall a length of corridor led up to the dining-room, reached by a flight of half a dozen steps. Doors to the pantry and store room opened off the passage and it was lit by a skylight opposite the pantry.

The store-room was a pleasant, spicy-smelling place, furnished with cupboards full of china and with open shelves. We used it as a flower room as well as for household stores. Its mullioned window looked out on the Kitchen-yard and under it stood the great stone jars in wicker jackets used for the annual vintage of sloe gin. During the weeks that followed the sloe gin's concoction, before the final processes of straining, bottling and corking, it was the duty of each member of the family entering the room to give the jars a thorough shaking.

The store-room proffered a delicious blend of appetising smells, for here my Mother kept her housekeeping supplies. Once in each quarter one of the farm waggons, the team decked out with all their ribbons and brasses and with the "rumblers" gaily chiming in their frame above the shaft mare's collar, would journey over the hill to Wareham station and bring back a full load of cases from the Army and Navy Stores. We—not unwillingly—were pressed into the important business of unpacking the cases, checking their contents by the invoices and stowing the goods away in their appointed places. Huge packages of candied peel, sultanas, raisins, currants, almonds, sugar—loaf, candied, demarara, crystallised, moist, caster, granulated, icing—of coffee, tea and cereals were opened and decanted into earthenware or tin containers. The 7-lb. tins of biscuits filled the space behind the door from floor to ceiling and regiments of jam-pots, bottles and jars were ranged in order on the shelves. All kinds of sauces, pickles and condiments, crystallised fruits and skins of glazing, pastes, potted meats and spices, nutmegs, chillis, isinglass, sardines and anchovies took their accustomed places. Chests on the floor accommodated soap and candles, brushes, dusters, swabs and floor cloths, blacking, polishes and knife powder, with leathers, saddle soap and sponges for the stable. I took some time, when I was married, to get accustomed to the hand-to-mouth idea of housekeeping in town, which still appears to me improvident and wasteful. The full shelves of the Tyneham store-room gave a sense of orderly preparedness and, save for stock-taking and ordering once a quarter, there was no need to worry about shopping, the constantly recurring burden of to-day.

My younger sister and I were given the corner of a shelf for our ferrets' gear and took great pride in keeping it in order. The bottles of ferret medicine and bright new feeding-tins stood neatly aligned, with collars, muzzles, lines and hedgers' gloves on hooks above.

On winter evenings, after lessons were done, we sometimes occupied ourselves with catching the store-room mice in a trap of our own devising. This was a 7-lb. biscuit tin with a strip of tissue paper laid across the open top and a piece of cheese adroitly balanced on the slender bridge. The nice adjusting of the paper and the exact amount of cheese which, plus the weight of a mouse, would cause the bridge to collapse at the critical moment, were only arrived at after many trials and failures, but after awhile we grew more expert and could account for several mice in quick succession. I think that seven was the record for one evening's work. One of my juvenile ambitions was to possess a pair of mouseskin gloves, but the preparation of the tiny squares of fur was a tedious business and the gloves were never achieved. I did however make myself a satisfying mouse-skin table mat and treasured it for many years.

The little set of steps from the dining-room was pleasant to jump down and still more pleasant to jump up with a running start from the hall end of the passage. The whole house might have been expressly planned for the delight of children, with all its long, wide passages and shallow stairs, providing plenty of room for exercise and play on stormy days.

The dining-room lay east and west, looking out to the south across the terraced flower garden to the hanging West Plantation, and to the east across the lawn and haha to the avenue.

A beautiful Sheraton sideboard with elegant brass railings stood facing the south windows and, near the fireplace, half a dozen shelves displayed a set of crested pewter plates as well as a few smaller table pieces, survivors of the ancient dinner service. The heavier plates and dishes had been relegated to the cellar.

In Uncle John's time every available corner of the room was crammed with books, including the one volume in the house accessible to us children which we cared to read:—"The Life of Stephen Hawker of Morwenstow", with a faded photograph of that fascinating worthy stuck inside the cover as a frontispiece. His life-long warfare with the Cornish wreckers and his loving care of his parishioners impressed us less than his eccentricities, the scarlet gloves he wore when in the pulpit and the nineteen cats who followed him to church and sat about the chancel while he preached. Another book in the dining-room with the attractive title "The Owlet of Owlstone Edge", proved a bitter disappointment, though I remember opening it on many occasions in the recurring hope of finding it more entertaining than it had seemed before.

Family portraits, of all manner of dates and varying degrees of artistry, looked down from the light green walls, and a fine, unfinished Gainsborough copy of Rubens' Antwerp altar-piece "The Descent from the Cross", in a magnificent contemporary frame, hung over the chimney-piece. The Kit-Kat portraits of my great-great-grandfather, John of Tyneham and Grange, and of his young son William, a fair-haired urchin in an amusing mulberry-coloured doublet slashed with pink, were very indifferent copies of the miniatures. John's picture was accompanied by his wife's and by portraits, deplorably inartistic but endearing, of his infant uncles, Thomas, afterwards of the Inner Temple, pleasantly posed in a deep blue-velvet coat, with long gold ringlets and a miniature dress sword, and Denis, rector-to-be of

Steeple-cum-Tyneham, frocked in crimson and buff and holding a tethered (or stuffed?) canary on his outstretched finger.

Above them hung the portrait of a Williams ancestor, Sir John, of Herringston, a ruffed and bearded Elizabethan whose tomb and massive monument are in S. Peter's, Dorchester, and a small painting of Leonora Sophia, daughter of Sir William Dutton Colt of the rose-diamond miniature and wife of Denis Bond of Grange. This lady's mother was a daughter of the Garneys family of Boyland Hall in Norfolk and of Kenton Hall in Suffolk and was co-heir to these proper-ties with her brother. A godchild of the ill-fated, uncrowned queen of George the First she received and bequeathed that poor princess' name to five successive generations.

In a shadowy corner hung the likeness, draped in heavy widow's weeds, of Mary, daughter of Lewis Williams of Shitterton and widow of Thomas Browne of Frampton. She married secondly Nathaniel Bond of Lutton, Serjeant-at-Law, so laying the foundation of the long connection between Tyneham and the family of Williams. She is alleged to have been a servant beater—perhaps no great distinction in the seventeenth century—and certainly her looks did not belie her reputation. The charming portrait of her little daughter Betty Browne, at play with a frisky dog, is in the dining-room at Grange. It was Mary's brother, Thomas, who left the entertaining notes which, under the title:—"Pocket Books of a Dorset Man, 1688-1701", formed the subject of a paper read before the Dorset Natural History and Archaeo-logical Society by my brother, and printed in volume 62 of the Society's Proceedings.

Great-uncle Tom, the genealogist, put up the stained glass window* on the staircase to commemorate the Serjeant and his wife. The gay heraldic colours of its armorial bearings and the clear inscription: "Nathaniel Bond, serviens domini regis ad legem, et Maria Williams, uxor ejus", greeted our eyes a dozen times a day as we ran past it to the schoolroom.

Among the remaining portraits there was one of another Williams, "Jack" of Herringston, a rubicund and jovial gentleman whose daughter Margaret married John the First of Tyneham. The almost full length picture of my mother sitting sketching in a beechwood was the last addition to the portrait gallery. She sat for it soon after her engagement and Hicks, the painter, was enchanted with his subject. He wished to paint her with her splendid red-gold hair hanging loose, but his proposal scandalised the elders of her family. Thwarted, the artist lost all interest in his work and painted my poor mother with her lovely hair scraped back and tightly plaited round her head. Her hair was always thick and wavy, reaching to her knees in glowing masses. In her old age the brightness of it faded but it never lost its colour and, in the last and ninety-eighth year of her life, her gentle face with its

---

*Now in the library of the Dorset County Museum.

delicate complexion, was still becomingly framed in braids of reddish gold.

The dining room had been the Kitchen of the original house but when my father's grandfather settled down at Tyneham in the first decade of the nineteenth century, he found the timbers of the roof in a dangerous condition and pulled the room down to rebuild it as it stands to-day. The original Kitchen had a seven-lighted mullioned window to the south and the great open fireplace which was moved to its present position in the hall of the fourteenth century building. According to a family tradition the roof space of the ancient house was used for keeping partridges, caught up and fattened among stooks of corn until needed for the table. A spiral staircase from the Kitchen to the Partridge Room is said to have occupied what is now the north-west corner of the dining-room.

CHAPTER II

Upstairs

THE central staircase to the upper floors was one of the chief architectural features of the house.

Beginning at the junction of the entrance stairs and passage to the dining-room it rose in wide and shallow steps, each cut from a single block of stone, round a square core of masonry, with ample landings at each turning.

On the first of these a door shut off the flight of steep stone steps descending to the Kitchen. There were no service stairs above this door until the landing by the Serjeants' window was arrived at.

From the next landing the west wing branched off to the left and here, too, was the entrance to the Porch Room with its own little set of rising steps inside the door. This part of the stairs was lighted by a high, south window with heraldic glass.

At the third turning, facing the Serjeants' window stood the grandfather clock whose chiming set the time for the whole house.

The square-cored stairway rose in four more sections to the top of the house. In these the solid stone of the steps gave place to well scrubbed deal. The rooms of the east front and south wing were reached by a corridor branching off to the left by the Serjeants' window. The stone stairs had the great advantage, to our youthful minds, of silence to the tread. No treacherous creak betrayed our farings to and fro on secret, all-important enterprises. In after years I came to appreciate the kindness of those easy steps to the old and lame.

In Tudor times the west wing probably contained one spacious chamber only, later divided into the two north rooms. The two rooms facing south were added by my great-grandfather when he rebuilt the dining-room. The bedrooms of the younger generation lay on either side of a passage ending in a window with a roomy window-seat, framing winter sunsets whose resplendent skies glowed through the tree stems of the Rookery Wood, with now and then a gleam of shining sea.

Both the north rooms were panelled and had ancient mullioned windows, again with comfortable window-seats. These rooms had such low doorways that we had to bend to enter them when we grew up. They both had spacious built-in bookshelves filled with books. The view from the windows through the trees to the Cowleaze Knap and distant hill was a blissful sight to awake to when the early sunlight touched the hillside long before it reached the valley, staining the tawny grass in summer or the frosted slopes in winter wonderful shades of apricot and rose.

The North Room, at the passage end, possessed an added attraction in the cheerful noises of the stable yard, beginning early with the sounds of grooming as the horses had their curry-combing done in the open air. The clank of bucket handles when the heavy wooden buckets were set down, the ring of iron shoes on the smooth stone setts, the coachman's steady hissing as he brushed and polished and the horses' gentle splutterings and blowings, rose up to the open window with their welcome message of another busy country day begun.

Steps in the thickness of the wall connected Uncle John's room with its neighbour, the small Porch Room. The space between the doors at top and bottom of the stairs had been converted to a cupboard where my mother kept her stationery stores.

The last room in the passage, looking seawards, was my younger brother's when he was at home, but was occupied by me in his lengthy absences at school, at Oxford and in the Sudan. Its window had an agreeable outlook on the dog yard, scene of perpetual comings and goings between the Kitchen yard and outside world. The tradesmen's carts and vans came in through the opening between the house and stables, and the odd man constantly plied, whistling, to and fro between the boiler rooms, the oil and coal sheds and the woodhouse. On rainy days the soothing sound of sawing told where gardeners and woodman were engaged on the indoor task of laying up stocks of logs and firewood for the winter. The lofty sycamores and elms in the Rookery Wood overtopped the buildings round the yard and formed the background of my view. The clamour of the rookery began and closed the day from early spring till autumn, when our Tyneham rooks, in company with all the other nesting colonies in the valley, departed to the "royal rookery" at Warmwell every afternoon, returning with the morning to their Purbeck feeding grounds and empty nurseries.

Half-way along the passage stood the door of the room whose occupant for many years was Hannah Hurworth, our beloved nurse.

One of the few south bedrooms in the house it looked across the kitchen-yard to the weathered stones and roof tiles of the oldest portion of the house and the flight of well-worn steps ascending to its flat arched entrance. Virginia creeper draped the walls and sprawled about the roof and chimneys, making a glorious splash of colour to old Hannah's annual delight.

The room eventually became my nephew's but I can never think of it without recalling Hannah seated by the window in her big armchair, her hands incessantly busied with her needlework or knitting, for she could never bear a moment's idleness.

Her loving welcome formed so large a part of every homecoming that Tyneham seemed half empty after she had gone. We sought her room a dozen times a day to ask advice or tell her of our doings and found her sympathy and interest never-failing. She was a Durham woman, born at Gainford on the Yorkshire border, and endowed with all the finest qualities of the north—thrift, industry and independence —with lofty principles and standards too often outraged by the slacker, slovenly ways of southerners. She came to us when I was less than two years old, and a contemporary portrait shows her as a tall, spare, handsome woman forty years old, with black hair smoothly parted, a strong, determined mouth and keen dark eyes. My mother found her frightening and austere at first and dreaded her free tongue, but very soon both parents' admiration and respect was won by Hannah's sterling character and devotion to her charges. I cannot remember being afraid of her myself, though she was strong on discipline, insisting on immediate and unquestioning obedience. Sometimes she spoke to us sharply and on occasion threatened execution "with the back of the hairbrush". But that was very seldom and the memories of tender comfortings are legion. She was a tower of refuge in all times of illness and distress and her beloved and loving children never grew too old to enjoy her cosseting or to appreciate her forthright criticisms of their looks or doings. She was a diligent reader, digesting what she read, thinking things out and forming her own opinions, to be held with firm conviction. I like to think of her as she was in our nursery walks, strolling along the lanes revolving problems in her mind and talking them out quietly with herself while keeping a watchful eye upon our scamperings. The habit of talking, *sotto voce*, to herself remained with her to the end and her low murmur as she sat in the evening by the nursery fire was a reassuring sound to a child in the darkened room next door. Sometimes another sound accompanied her voice for, when it grew too dark for needlework, she would take up a pack of cards and shuffle them to occupy her ever restless fingers. She was a person of strong antipathies and sympathies, reserving most of her affections for her own and her adopted families. Where she gave her love she was completely selfless and ready to sacrifice herself without reserve. She was intolerant of any scamping or departure from her own high moral standards but I do not think she ever complained of a fellow-servant or passed on what she heard in the "hall". As she grew old both manner and appearance softened, but to the end she held herself erect and kept her dignity of bearing. In her latter years she was given the charge of all the household linen and kept it exquisitely mended. She was, too, made responsible for the dessert, a task assigned in the hope of drawing her away from her interminable sewing. She thoroughly enjoyed her expeditions to the garden and, loving nature, liked to be out-of-doors, but could not long be parted from her needle. She would not let me buy my trousseau and made it all herself with the finest of tucks and embroidery and almost invisible stitches. Within a few days of her death, with mind and sight both gone, her worn and feeble hands still plucked at the sheets with the motions of sewing a seam.

She saved up a large sum of money, stowed away for the most part in cupboards and boxes, and was urged by her kinsfolk to give up her work and spend her last years in retirement at Gainford. More than once she made up her mind to go back to the north, but when the time came for the parting her heart always failed her. She could not envisage life far from Tyneham and those whom she cherished and loved as her own.

She was the type of all those loved and faithful family friends and servants whose honoured names run like a golden thread through the stuff of my happiest memories. I recognise now how blest were the children of my generation who were subject to old-fashioned nannies with loving and strict rules of discipline. Poor babes who have never known the peace and safe routine of nursery life !

This poor description of a noble and outstanding personality does little justice to her sterling character. It is, at least, an effort to pay tribute to her faithful service as well as an expression of undying gratitude for a devotion which can never be repaid.

Next door to Hannah's bedroom a deep cupboard in the passage was her private glory hole where she hoarded cardboard boxes, paper, bags of string and a surprising store of oddments. She would triumphantly produce all kinds of unexpected treasures from its dark recesses to supply some far-fetched need of family or guests.

The Porch Room, an odd little L-shaped chamber, occupied the space above the entrance hall. Its long side lay between the door and the mullioned window over the north porch and here my writing-table stood, in a bracing draught. The short stroke of the L contained the fireplace and my mother's kneehole desk, the hub round which the life of the house revolved. I fear that in the manner of the young we took our wellbeing very much for granted and it was long before we realised how much the comfort and harmonious working of the household hung upon my mother's forethought and continual care.

The Porch Room was a snug and cheerful little place in spite of its northern aspect. My younger brother's Japanese and Chinese prints and water colours covered the wall, and finches and canaries chirped and sang in their window cages, for my mother was an ardent lover of birds.

The doorway of the Porch Room was still lower than the lintels of the west wing bedrooms, and the entrance stairway, tunnelled through the four foot thickness of the wall, was a trap for tall and unsuspecting strangers.

Beyond the Porch Room landing two more flights of the central stairway rose to the level of the east front bedrooms. These, like the rooms in the west wing, may once have formed a single chamber reached by a door beside the Serjeants' window, though possibly the Chintz Room was divided from the rest. In later times the space was cut up into four apartments and a passage.

The Chintz Room, illustrated in the article on Tyneham which appeared in *Country Life*, still had its Tudor panelling, carved frieze and a chimney piece of slightly later date. This is the woodwork now set up in memory of my brother in the County Museum. Two mullioned windows of three lights apiece were set breast high in the walls to north and east. The northern one contained two ancient roundels of stained glass from Boyland Hall, the Garneys' home in Norfolk, one with the arms of Garneys and of Tyrrel and the motto :—"Goddes Grace Governe Garneys", the other bearing a coat and motto made illegible by time. This window and the stained glass in the library below were damaged while the W.A.A.F's inhabited the house in 1943. Fire drill was ordered and the girls descended a rope ladder from the attic window in the Chintz Room gable, a window walled up in the days of window tax but opened as a fire escape by the R.A.F. Nothing was done to protect the lower windows from the swinging ladder and the damage done went unreported. The scattered fragments of stained glass were lost before my brother could attempt to save them. The Garneys window had a very old iron fastening, simple, graceful and ingenious, of which there is a drawing in the County Museum. All windows in the house were furnished with stout shutters, effective against winter draughts and cold. In my great-uncle's time the upstairs rooms had old white dimity curtains all alike. I took some spare ones to my new home, forty years ago, and still possess them sound and good as new. There was a spacious cupboard in the thickness of the wall beside the chimney breast, packed with all kinds of medical stores. A large proportion of them dated from pre-telegraph days when, with the nearest doctor living at Corfe, a good five miles away "by horse", first aid materials and homely treatments were essential and the house must be able to produce them as the need arose. Guests new to the Chintz Room and expecting to find wardrobe space behind the cupboard door were disconcerted when confronted by the piles of lint and cottonwool, the boxes full of bandages, the vaporising kettle for small sufferers from croup and "bronical" complaints, the quantities of well-proved remedies—among them the infallible quinsy cure from my mother's Yorkshire home—the bottles of disinfectants, carron oil for burns, the cough cures, camphorated oil and embrocations, finger stalls and eye shades. When I was young, before communication with the outside world became so easy, there was seldom a week without a messenger appearing at the door to ask for aid in some emergency or illness. My mother or Hannah often went in person with the remedies if help or advice seemed called for. The cupboard held Wincarnis and malt extract, meat essences and Parrish's Food to help the village convalescents. Some of the sufferers still preferred their own traditional cures. Cobwebs were often used for staunching wounds without any apparent ill effects. Dandelion tea was a popular concoction and so was nettle tea, especially in the spring.

I had a special liking for the Chintz Room dressing-room and occupied it on my visits to Tyneham after I left home. Only a small square of the leaded window could be opened and it, too, still possessed its original fastening, a toothed arrangement less efficient than the

Chintz Room spring, in fact completely useless in a wind. But the first sunshine touched this window and, at all hours of the day, it had a perfect outlook on the Avenue and up the steep slope of the Hole Field to the hanging wood, with all their lively traffic of animals and birds. The gulls began it in the hour before the dawn, screaming and clamouring far up in the sky as they passed in full cry to their inland feeding grounds, and the last sounds at nightfall were the cushioned voices of the ring doves in the limes. On stormy days a missel thrush would shout his ringing challenge from the top of the tall chestnut on the lawn and the first thrush and blackbird songs of springtime came from the Hole Field thickets and the garden shrubberies. Chiffchaffs and willow warblers, tits, woodpeckers and nuthatches were noisy in the Avenue and orchard. Ravens, peregrines and jackdaws passed over many times a day, swifts from the cliffs wove patterns across the sky, a pair of buzzards mewed above their nest in a silver fir behind the orchard, and barn and tawny owls plied to and from their homes in the hollow sycamores of the terrace garden. The choughs had disappeared from Gadcliff long before my time but remained emblazoned in the Williams arms in house and church. The steady rise and fall of the nightjar's spinning-wheel note made a pleasant background to the earlier summer evenings of my childhood and I remember one pair nesting in the Lower Horse Close Belt. Later they disappeared and came no more for many years until my brother heard them once again in 1940. Sometimes a pair of stock doves settled in the Great Wood for the summer months and the monotonous purr of turtle doves accompanied the drowsy afternoons.

The cows which kept the House supplied with milk grazed the West Mead, Hole Field and Avenue until my father took the farm in hand. Then the House dairy was closed down and the home fields were left to the 'odd' horse, "Punch" and his successors, a dynasty of cobs and ponies and our trotting donkey, "Blitz". The ring of iron shoes on stones, the yap of a fox or the hooting of an owl were the only sounds which broke the silence round the House by night. The panels of the dressing-room were hung with dark engravings of unequal merit but endeared by long acquaintance. This room and my father's shared a chimney, with fireplaces aslant across a corner.

My father's bedroom, a facsimile of the Chintz Room dressing-room, contained an amusing dressing table of cream-painted Chippendale—one of the many pieces of its period and kind at Tyneham—made on the slant to fit the window recess.

My mother's bedroom occupied the south-east angle of the house and, like the Chintz Room, was cross-lighted by two breast-high windows with wide sills. This White Room had been set apart as a study for Uncle John and had a porch with double doors to keep out noise—one wonders now what noise could possibly have threatened to disturb him in those quiet years ?—but I have no remembrance of its use by him and when, as children, we looked in through its seldom open door, not venturing to set foot beyond the threshold, it had an air of calm detachment, as if it carried on a quiet and secret life of its own when the door was closed. A stiff array of chairs encircled a central table furnished with piles of books in a formal pattern like the spokes of a wheel, with a hawfinch, stuffed and under a domed glass shade, for the hub.

My mother, when she took the White Room for her own, retained the pictures as she found them and was surrounded by some charming groups of seascapes and a few engravings hung against the pale blue panelling. The window on the south side, framed by the glossy, tan-lined leaves of the giant magnolia, gave a bird's-eye view of the terraced garden. How often I have seen my mother in contented contemplation of her handiwork and how many times been called into consultation at the window over plans for the rearrangement of her borders.

Outside the White Room porch the corridor turned first to the west and then to the south again towards the two South Rooms. A big sash window opened from it to the leads about the lantern skylight. When there were house or dinner-parties we as children climbed out on the leads to watch the couples going in procession along the lamplit corridor below. My father seldom failed to look up and smile, pointing us out to the leading lady on his arm. To dine out in the country must have needed courage in those days before the advent of the car, while low-cut evening dresses with long trains were still *de rigeur*. Most people had too much consideration for their stablemen to take them out at night without sufficient cause and, where the party was within a walk, the guests would drive themselves in an open trap or go on foot. The rector's wife trudged up across the muddy fields, goloshed and wrapped in shawls and cloaks above her tucked-up satin dress. A whaleboned hood protected her coiffure but, even so, on windy nights her hair required adjustment on arrival and a room was set at her disposal, warmed by a good coal fire and lit with candles. We thought it a great treat to be allowed to help her change into her satin shoes and to watch her putting finishing touches to the sparkling garnet ornaments in her hair.

It was just before the outbreak of the first World War that my father put a heating system in the house and made the alterations to the store room and the pantry. He added bathrooms in this first-floor passage as well as ample linen and drying cupboards.

The two South Rooms above the dining-room lay at a higher level than the rest of the first floor, at the top of a flight of stairs. First came the room apportioned to the governess and then, through a short dark entry to the right, the schoolroom. In Dr. Sauer's tenancy, soon after my father's death, these rooms were thrown into one and the eastern window, blocked to avoid the window tax, reopened, making a charming sunny bedroom.

Apart from winter draughts and cold the schoolroom in our day was a cheerful, comfortable place and we enjoyed the view it gave us of the flower garden, backed by Eweleaze and Great Wood, affording us a variety of nice distractions during lessons.

The soothing sounds of scythe and mowing-machine in the summer term, the brushing of crisp leaves on autumn days, and the chink of hoes on gravel paths, the small talk of the rooks and, at all seasons of the year, the brittle chime of sheep bells, mixed harmoniously with scales and recitations. To glance up from our books was to see the sheep or cattle grazing in the field, sometimes a hare or fox or roedeer passing between garden and Plantation and, on one memorable day, a snow-white stoat on the track of a luckless rabbit in the rowaty grass. The stoat in its ermine coat is now in the County Museum. I cannot remember our dear Russian governess, Anna Petrovna Sokolova, showing any annoyance at my running away from studies in so worthy a cause, and indeed she showed her sympathy with all our interests and pursuits, encouraging us in them as long as they did not interfere too much with schoolroom work. She was as fond of animals as we were and never objected to their presence in the schoolroom, so that we worked, as a rule, with a couple of dogs asleep by the fire and a cat on each lap at the round centre table. Old photographs of former pupils, friends and Russian kinsfolk crowded chimney-piece and bookshelves, a strange and alien people to our eyes, the men with hair *en brosse* and bushy beards, their frock or uniform coats ablaze with medals and orders, the ladies charming and romantic with their soft dark eyes and braided hair worn high like coronets. We knew their histories and idiosyncrasies to the smallest detail, though thinking of them as queer denizens of a remote and only half real world.

"Socky" herself was typically Slav in her appearance though of mixed descent, her father (as she never tired of telling us) of the *haute noblesse* of Russia and her mother an operatic singer of distinction, a German from the Baltic Provinces. Their daughter's face was round, high cheekboned, with a pugnacious nose and dark short-sighted eyes. She was exceptionally gifted and intelligent, a conscientious teacher anxious to pass on her knowledge. But, to her, moral values and good manners were of greater consequence than learning gained from books and she visited our failures in our lessons with less severity than she showed towards lapses from the code of courtesy or honour. "Socky" spoke French, Russian, German and English equally well. I shall always be sorry that I made no better use of her talent as a linguist. Her literary taste was excellent and she contrived to hammer into us a measure of appreciation of the best in English, French and German letters. Shakespeare she idolised and knew his plays a good deal better than the average educated Englishman can claim to do. She made us read and study them, committing lengthy passages to unwilling memories. She was a competent pianist and a good teacher of the piano and, though she did not draw, she did her utmost to encourage my small taste in drawing. I think she enjoyed the two or three occasions when she went with me to Calderon's School of Animal Painting held at

Liphook for a fortnight in the summer. The other students, all a good deal older than myself, regarded her as something in the way of light relief to their serious work and I was deeply mortified by being so strictly chaperoned in a world where chaperons were unknown. I spent three days a week of two Lent terms at Calderon's School off Baker Street, and poor long-suffering "Socky" appeared at luncheon intervals to take me out for fish and chips at an Italian restaurant nearby. She caused unseemly merriment by her entrance into the studio in her high-perched toque, glaring her disapproval of its atmosphere through the pince-nez which were always slipping off and needing readjusting. She happily seemed unaware of the amusement she was causing, but I was deeply conscious of it and, detesting all my graceless fellow-students, suffered miseries on her behalf.

My parents held her in affection and esteem but must have found her something of a trial now and then. She had strong views on nearly every subject and rejoiced in argument. She sided fiercely with the Boers in the South African War and took no pains to hide her satisfaction at a British reverse, which made things difficult for us who had a son and brother fighting with our forces. But I have often wondered whether her contrariness in always taking the opposing view was just a means of bringing interest and excitement into a somewhat lonely life. She loved the Coppice Walk, which my father called her "quarter deck", and spent long hours pacing-up and down it, practising scales and operatic airs or talking vehemently to herself in a variety of languages. Her garden, a small square adjoining our little plots, gave her great delight and, for the rest, when not with us she wrote long letters to her niece in Germany, knitted and mended, read, played and sang. She tried, at my mother's behest, to make us competent needlewomen. I am sorry to confess that her success was small, though we blackened seams and stabbed our fingers every Saturday while she read aloud from a book of Greek mythology. The "Myths of Hellas" did stick in our minds, for which I owe her gratitude. It was many years, however, before I finally identified the whole of the oddly-sounding names, as "Socky" pronounced them, with the Anglicised divinities and heroes met with later on in print.

Between the Russian Anna and the Durham Hannah a polite relationship existed, lacking warmth or sentiment and founded on reciprocal respect, but the domestic staff with few exceptions gave our poor "Socky" just as little deference as they dared. I have often thought that the hardest part of the Victorian governess' lot must have been the cruelty of servants. Perpetual warfare raged between the kitchen and the schoolroom. Though "Socky" shared our breakfast, luncheon and tea as a matter of course, her supper was sent up to her in the schoolroom and this was a perennial grievance with the cooks. My mother might be deep in accounts or correspondence before dinner when poor "Socky", flushed and voluble, would burst into the Porch Room with her supper dish, demanding an inspection of the "dogs' food *diese unverschämte Köchin*" had been impudent enough to send up as an evening meal. Only long and tactful soothing and a promise that the matter would be dealt with in the morning could persuade the injured Russian to retire with the offending dish. She could be heard returning to the schoolroom, still muttering in several tongues, leaving my mother with the prospect of a painful interview with an already mutinous and resentful cook.

The South Room did not catch the full force of the south-west wind as badly as did some parts of the house but, when it was blowing hard, the thunderous roar of the gale in the West Plantation made a sound as of rushing water which puzzled and frightened guests new to it. The valley acted as a funnel for the wind and when the winter gales came storming up from the sea the noise they made was awe-inspiring even to those who knew the strength and thickness of the walls. In the brief lulls between the gusts the tempest could be heard a mile away approaching from the Bay, threshing and bullying the tormented trees until with a roar like a clap of thunder the full force of it struck the house and made it shudder from the shock. It often seemed as if the frail old casements must give way before the onslaught of the blasts.

A door on the landing by the Serjeant's window shut away the four last turnings of the square-cored stairway. In these, the stone of the steps gave place to deal and it was on this staircase that there lingered the entrancing smell of the Tyneham of our childhood, long after it had faded from the rest of the house. The essence of it may have been the wholesome smell of well-scrubbed floor boards left, in the uncle's time, uncovered here as in the passages and bedrooms. Other ingredients, such as lavender, old furniture and a certain shut-up dampness must have entered into it, resulting in a haunting and elusive scent peculiar to the house for I have never come across its like elsewhere. One whiff of it, if I could smell it again, would I am certain take me back across the years and I should be a child again with Tyneham quiet and homely as I knew and loved it then. No restless or unhappy ghost had then disturbed the ancient house's peace. It was impossible to picture scenes of violence in the friendly rooms. They held the memories of so many quiet lives lived out between their walls, of deep affections, kindly services performed, of sorrows and pain transformed by faith to peace.

I suppose that strangers might have been impressed by the general shabbiness of paint and furnishings. Carpets and curtains, chair covers and bed hangings all had served their turn for generations. Original colours may have been improved by age and wear, at any rate they had reached a stage where their several colours blended softly and harmoniously. The idea of Tyneham rooms decked out with spick and span upholsteries, however "period" or artistic, appears incongruous to my mind.

Mounting the stairs one came at the second turning to the little sunken doorway leading to the men's rooms over the west wing. The footman's room was long and low, housing along one side of it such bulky treasures as the brass-nail-studded boxes made to fit the travelling-carriages' curves, and the cowhide-covered box which went with Onesiphorus Bond to school in the 1640's. There, too, were the wig boxes of our forebears and the trunks in which were folded away the clothes they wore. Among these were an enchanting suit of rich, dark velvet, the colour of a purple Orleans plum, with silver-buttoned coat and breeches, worn by my father's grandfather in his youth, and an oyster satin waistcoat, believed to have belonged to the "common ancestor", with exquisite embroidery of flowers in multi-coloured silks. Another box held rapiers and dress swords*.

Beyond this room, a door and narrow passage led into the butler's lair, a smaller edition of the footman's room, distinguished by an ancient four-post bed hung round with the inevitable dimity curtains. From both these rooms, as well as from the attics facing east, low doors in the walls gave access to vast spaces under the roof, most tempting to exploring minds, but enterprise in this direction was discouraged by authority. The hollow walls and roof space harboured hordes of rats, whose nightly junketings outdid the noisiest of hauntings. The proper ghostly noises were all there, knockings and whimperings, clank of what seemed like chains, the thud of heavy objects being dropped and the swish of silken skirts. At times, in my early years, the rats came out into the passages and scampered to and fro, gnawing the panelling and doors in emulation of those mice which, as a Berkshire friend once told me, tried "to barricade their way" into her hen-house.

At the head of the staircase lay what we as children called the Throne Room, a little bedroom almost wholly occupied by steps which culminated, in the centre of the floor space, in a platform only just large enough to accommodate the bed. This was the scullery-maid's apartment and how we envied her for being lodged in such a fascinating and unusual chamber. I have wondered, since, how it struck a new arrival introduced into her bower, and how many falls she took before she grew accustomed to the surprising ledges of her bedroom floor. Beyond the Throne Room was a passage corresponding to the first-floor corridor, with four rooms to the east and one, a modern addition made in 1914, looking west. The room over the Chintz Room was held sacred to the cook, the next was shared by kitchenmaid and under housemaid, its neighbour was inhabited by the upper housemaid and the fourth by my mother's maid in latter days. In the great uncle's time and earlier still it was the nursery. We loved it for its clean, bare whiteness and for the view of lawn and avenue from the lofty window-seat. It had the pleasant Tyneham smell in fullest measure, laced with a

---

* The mens' suits, with a Stuart stump-work box and a Jacobean needlework curtain, are now in the County Museum.

flavouring of tallow dip and of seaweed trophies brought back from the shore. An empty coconut was hung from the centre of the ceiling, a relic of my father's and his brother's and sister's nursery days. It gave the attic its name and, for all I know, still hangs in the Coconut Room.

The new west attic was the best room of them all and was appropriated by the married couple who fulfilled the roles of parlourman and head-housemaid-cum-lady's-maid after the dynasties of lady's maids and butlers had become extinct.

Most of the painted Chippendale pieces in the house were of the same design and colour, cream with thin black outlines to panels, drawers and, in the case of chairs, to slats and legs, but at the top of the stairs outside the Throne Room stood a chest-of-drawers which showed a departure from the prevailing pattern—its groundwork was a deeper shade of cream, picked out with Indian red and either blue or green.

The charming period furniture had to a large extent retreated upwards to the attic floor before my memories of the house begin, but many of the old rush-bottomed chairs and some of the tables still adorned the bedrooms, and Hannah's room contained a graceful chest-of-drawers with cupboard top. I think there was another in the cook's room and a larger edition of them in the housekeeper's room.

According to my brother Ralph the attics looking east were almost certainly one long and unpartitioned space originally and were only cut up into separate rooms in 1820. During the "occupation" of the house in 1944, the Royal Air Force, with my brother's consent, took down the dividing walls to make a dormitory.

These servants' quarters were to my mind remarkably good for the period of the house, or indeed, for any period. They were protected from extremes of temperature by ample roof space topped with thick stone tiles. They had no central heating, it is true, but neither had the lower regions of the house until just before the 1914 war. The servants had no bedroom fires in winter time (no more had we), but neither had they fires in their rooms at home.

The critics of accommodation offered to domestic servants half a century ago forget perhaps that the age was hardier and less self-indulgent and that all sections of society were far less pampered than they are to-day. Except in a few luxurious palaces of the ultra-rich the standard of ease and comfort was far lower and employers cheerfully did without a number of refinements now considered necessary in the smallest council house. Rightly or wrongly, money spent on personal comfort was considered an extravagance, and discipline, self-imposed, had not yet gone completely out of fashion. My brothers wore no gloves, however cold the weather, and none of us possessed a warm top coat until a voyage undertaken in the winter, after I grew up, induced the purchase of this thin end of a wedge. My mother would not countenance hot-water bottles except when we were ill, and I whose toes were rarely anything but cold endured a quantity of comfortless and wakeful hours in consequence. In winter we would warm our flannel petticoats by Hannah's fire, roll them up tightly, run back to our beds and wrap the flannel round our feet.

Until I was seventeen I was sent to bed on the stroke of eight o'clock and made my supper off a biscuit and a glass of milk. I wonder still at the amount of food small children can consume for supper and breakfast in these more enlightened times. My mother had another rule—an excellent one as I now see it—barring all nibbling and drinking between meals. In winter we had a "nammut" of hot milk or soup at 11 o'clock, and in summer, when we went to bathe, might take a pocketful of biscuits to the shore. Otherwise we had no such light refreshments and did not miss the frequent drinks, snacks, sweets and ices needed to sustain the spark of life in our successors.

No doubt the younger members of the household staff were sometimes put upon by "uppers" who treated them more autocratically than did their employers but, as regards the physical wellbeing of the youngsters, they had nothing to complain of. Regular meals of wholesome, well-cooked food soon showed results in rapid growth and healthier complexions. It was good to watch a child from a thriftless home filling out in a few weeks' time.

Hardship, if hardship did exist, was rarely due to the employer but rather to the petty tyranny of some upper servant, as has been said already. Domestic dignitaries on the whole were kind and well-intentioned, taking real trouble to instruct and help their underlings who often looked upon them as their best friends and advisers. The boys and girls, however, were taught to know their places in the little domestic world and had to learn the rules laid down by its most despotic of trades unions. A strict adherence to these regulations was a minor burden of employers who, like the latest joined recruit to the household's strength, must needs respect them. Each self-defined department kept to itself and would not do a stroke of work belonging to another except in case of illness, when the stringency of the law might be relaxed.

The younger generation's notion of domestic service in Victorian and Edwardian days has often made me smile. The times have changed so quickly and completely that contemporary writers can have had no personal experience of the conditions they describe, but there are surely sources full of first-hand knowledge easily to be tapped. In spite of this, in novel after novel, dream worlds appear in which the oddly balanced households seem to consist of kitchen and pantry staffs alone. A pompous butler and attendant parlourmaid, with some assistance from the cook's department, between them do the work of nonexistent housemaids. The parlourmaid appears to valet men as well as women guests. The "tweenie" of the novelist is an imaginary creature with peculiar tasks which I have known to include the answering of the drawingroom bell and even attendance on her mistress while she dresses for a ball. In real life this little Cinderella helped the housemaids after breakfast and then descended to the scullery where she stayed at the cook's behest for the rest of the day. Even in smaller households, as at Tyneham, outings were so arranged as to leave a representative of each department always on the spot.

Another unknown territory for mid-twentieth century writers is the coachman's realm of duties. The fictional coachman, like the private chauffeur, his successor, is made in novels to get down from his seat to open carriage doors, tuck rugs round his employer's knees or ring the doorbell, leaving his helpless cargo at the mercy of two uncontrolled and corn-fed horses which cannot be made immobile by putting them into neutral !

A footman at Tyneham went with the carriage when it was meeting visitors or on occasions when the coachman was alone, otherwise passenger members of the family got out to open gates, leave cards or do the shopping. The Tyneham coachman's job was not an ordinary or an enviable one. The distance into Wareham and nature of the road meant that the horses could not do the double journey twice in the day. So, when a member of the family was away all day, the pair must needs be housed for many hours at the "Red Lion" stables. These idle times with work undone at home and nowhere in town to spend the hours of waiting, must have been wearisome and galling for an active man. On reaching home, however late, his work was far from ended. The hasty locking of a garage door was not for him. The tired and muddied horses must be left to cool off slowly before they could be finished off and bedded down. In spite of drawbacks such as these the men with a love of horses would not have changed their work for any other. At home the coachman's job was snug enough in his horse-warmed stable or beside the saddle-room fire with the comforting companionship of horses and stable cats, backed by such homely sounds as the rustle of straw, the steady munching and the gentle sneeze when a nose was tickled by the hay, or the whirr of a head rope running through a ring each time its wearer turned his head or lowered it again into the manger.

Before the bathroom era water for the baths was carried to the bedrooms from the kitchen, as were the smaller quantities for washing before meals, in a regiment of cans, bright brass for the best rooms, painted for the rest. The slops from baths and basins had to be carried down again to the boxed-in sink below the window-seat at the end of the west wing passage. These daily tasks, together with the fires to be laid and lit in winter, made plenty of work for housemaids, but it must not be forgotten that, in those days, there was an indoor staff of nine, as well as an odd man. The thirty paraffin lamps which needed cleaning, trimming and refilling, every day, had two men in the pantry to contend with them.

In the early 1940's when my brother was living at Tyneham, the house was efficiently run by a cook and a houseman, with a boy in the kitchen and help now and then with the housework.

CHAPTER III

Kitchen and Outhouses

THE stone steps from the kitchen lobby to the staircase landing ran up side by side with a similar but shorter flight to the pantry. The former flight was steep and slippery and made descent in hob-nailed shoes a hazardous undertaking. The stone-flagged lobby at the bottom which received the casualties connected the back entrance with the kitchen premises.

Along the lobby wall the house bells hung in a row, each with coiled spring and metal crank above it and the name of its room in painted lettering below, though every bell possessed its readily distinguishable voice. The bell-wires must have been a complicated system and, when one was set in motion, its rattling and grating squeaks were audible in all the rooms along its route. Their merit lay in the fact that they never went out of order and that their functioning was not dependent on an evanescent battery. They could be recognised by their individual tongues or, failing that, by the plainly visible swinging of the bell itself, an advantage not possessed by their electrical successors with their one impersonal note and indicators whose faint quiverings are scarcely noticeable at a few yards distance.

The kitchen, like every well-planned kitchen, faced the north and had a long, high window overlooking the brewhouse. Its floor was flagged with stone and, when I remember it first, the fire was open. The joints of meat were roasted on a spinning jack inside a semi-circular metal screen with a well below to hold the basting-spoon and catch the dripping gravy. Meat baked in the oven, as it later came to be, was lacking in the juiciness and succulent flavour of those evenly cooked and constantly basted joints. Hams, home-cured, hung from the ceiling cased in muslin bags and a row of copper pans reflected firelight from their places on the wall.

A dark little tunnel on the left side of the hearth went through to scullery, larder and the housekeeper's room or cook's small parlour, tucked in the north-west angle of the house.

A long succession of cooks presided over the kitchen and their reigns, like the reigns of the kings of Israel, were sometimes evil, sometimes good. So much of the happiness and comfort of the household hinged on the character of the cook, and women like Fanny Stickland, Maggie Drew and Ada Burden somehow managed to create an atmosphere of peace and wellbeing felt throughout the house. A few were petty tyrants, making trouble from the first, so that we all rejoiced

27

when they departed at the earliest possible moment. One such, when the house was full on Christmas Eve, ran suddenly amok and chased the screaming kitchenmaid with a carving knife. The girl was rescued by the pantry staff, the cook disarmed and locked into her room to sober down, while frightened underlings set to and cooked the dinner with considerable success. My mother learned by dark experience to advertise for temporary cooks and this manoeuvre almost always proved successful. The cooks who took the situation as a permanency, alarmed when they realised the remoteness of their destination, as often as not gave notice on arrival, whereas the "temporaries", once having it made plain that nothing would induce them to remain for more than a month, took root in half that time and stayed for years.

The servants' hall or Staff Room (infelicitous term!) as it later became, lost the sunshine early in the afternoon. At night when the crimson curtains screened the window and a good fire blazed it was a cheerful room to sit in. The younger members of the staff spent lively hours round the centre table playing card and race games under the kindly supervision of the upper housemaid. Luncheon once over, cook retired to the seclusion of her room and was seen no more until she emerged refreshed, at six o'clock or so, to set about preparing dinner. The butler made for his home or, if a bachelor, sat down with pipe and papers in the pantry, while Hannah and my mother's maid sewed, each by preference in her personal domain and by her own warm hearth.

There were no evenings out, except where a young maid's home was near enough for her to spend her off time with her family, and then she would be escorted home by nine o'clock by father or brother. The girls could go out in the afternoons, to Worbarrow or the village, and some had bicycles to take them to the Wareham shops. The footmen fished or went off rabbiting with Henry Miller according to the season. I never heard the want of regular "outings" given as a reason for wanting a change. Conditions were the same, perhaps even stricter, in other country-houses and parents expected sons and daughters to be well looked after by employers. Young folk were not so restless and agog for entertainment out-of-doors as they are to-day. All people in the country, whatever their position, were content to find amusements by their own firesides and though we all looked forward to and enjoyed an occasional jollification, deriving from it plenty of unsophisticated pleasure, we were easily satisfied and made our entertainment out of very scant material.

Our parents never gave us expensive toys—they would have thought it an unjustified extravagance—and we certainly did not miss them. We had to use our own imaginations and inventiveness for games and this applied to the village children, too. I think we derived far more amusement from such simple sources than from any toys that money could have bought us.

Our outdoor range was limited by the capacity of our own legs or the donkey's, a radius large enough to hold a multitude of forms of entertainment. Allowing for the golden haze through which we view re-membered scenes of childhood, I still believe our self-contrived amusements made us happier than ready-made, elaborate playthings would have done. We played a form of hockey, fast and furious, with bent sticks and a discarded tennis ball, ran "drags" for the dogs with an ancient rabbitskin, or paper chases with a neighbouring family of girls of our own ages. On windy days we "sailed" with a rug stretched tight between two sticks, or raced our tam-o'-shanters on the Cowleaze Knap. We traced out labyrinths in the fallen lime leaves on the lawn, inventing games to play in them. We plaited wattle houses in the wood and acted serial plays about them as adventurers and explorers. The heavy trolley used for moving logs became a cherished plaything not without its hazards. We dragged it to the brow of the Cowleaze Knap, stood on it, steering by the handle-bar, and charged with gathering speed down the stony carriage drive and past the House to the stable plot. A specially thrilling feat was to negotiate the dog-leg turning into the steeper, more rewarding gradient of the back approach, but this too often ended in a head-on crash into the wall. A frequent agent of disaster was the loosening of the pin attaching handle-bar and trolley head, so that the pilot found herself without control over the machine and had to jump for life. Out little cousins never tired of playing with the "Tortoise" when they stayed at Tyneham and, long years after-wards, my brother's children resurrected it and put it into action once again. Compared with the heavy and unwieldy trolley our toboggan on wheels was, both in speed and streamline, as a race-horse is to a Suffolk Punch. It was a simple, home-made wooden affair, a narrow platform mounted on four six-inch solid wooden wheels, but it offered endless possibilities. We used it on the sharp descent at the end of the West Plantation, where the hill dropped steeply, cut across by narrow terraces or lynchets, an admirable run. The toboggan gathered speed from the moment it was launched and shot off into space from the brink of each successive ledge to land spine-rackingly on the next comparatively level stretch of grass. Molehills and clumps of grass and furze introduced exciting hazards and we could never understand why guests invited to form part of the crew were so unappreciative of the refinements of the course. Their cries were drowned by the deafening clatter of the wheels and, when they reached the end of the descent, they seldom seemed inclined to try it again. One of the few exceptions to the rule was Detmar Blow, who stayed with us while drawing plans for alter-ations to the House. Many years afterwards I learned from Lady Cynthia Asquith's "Haply I may remember" that he introduced the sport of wheel-tobogganing, with happy results, to the young Charteris' at Stanway.

Jumping afforded us perpetual sport and we had special jumping places in the furze brakes on the Knap as well as a measured gate of poles to put up in the garden. "I spy" round the rickyard and in the shuttered dairy house was pleasantly horrifying and productive of ensuing nightmares.

But for the most part we were satisfied with ordinary pleasures of the country, walks—more often runs—on the hills and in the fields, marking the plants and birds and insects, hunting for nuts and straw-berries, mushrooms, blackberries and earth-nuts, getting to know each tree and bush and stone as a loved, familiar friend. How thankful I have been, through more than half a lifetime spent in towns, for those good years of freedom in the clean, cool Purbeck air, with daily deepening of impressions gathered from the tranquil circling of the country seasons. Not only did they store the mind with countless scenes of beauty to draw upon in times of trouble or stress, but the peaceful, well-remembered background formed a steady anchorage for the spirit in a restless and unstable world. From our earliest years our parents made companions of us in their walks, pointing out everything of interest and teaching us the names of what we saw, so that in later life no journey through the country could lack interest and delight. Poor little 'bus-borne children, how I pity you, "missing so much and so much!" What can you know of England who only know its well-tarred roads and asphalt play-grounds, robbed as you are of your country heritage?

My father spent the whole day in the open with his field-glasses and spud, inspecting stock or plantings and directing the estate work while waging endless war against the thistles.

My mother, even in advanced old age, was an indefatigable walker. She felt the skies were falling if she had to miss her daily constitutional. At Tyneham in her seventies she still did men's work in the garden for long hours and then, when tea was over, sprang to her feet, exclaiming: "*Now* I must take some *exercise*. Who is coming for a walk?"

These—to me—pleasant reminiscences have led me far from the servants' hall which set them going.

Leaving it by the pantry stairs and lobby we come once more to the front of the house, descending the stone stairway to the north or entrance hall, a little rectangle pervaded by the camphory smell of carriage rugs and mounted heads, my father's "royal" stag, stalked at Glen Tanar, the then record sable antelope and a monster moose. Doors, right and left, shut off a closet and the cellar steps.

The cellar was dry though heavily festooned with black cotton-wool-like fungus and, in the haste of the evacuation in December 1943, its vaults were stacked with the more valuable and fragile of the furniture, locked up and sealed. At that time, at the height of the war, no warehouse could be found to take the contents of the house. My brother's wife applied in vain to fourteen firms. Much of the furniture was piled up in the brewhouse and Museum, Grange housed some in its laundry cottage, some found a temporary home at Winfrith Rectory and the books were heaped up in the new granary.

30

Later the Air Force lorries flattened the surface drains outside the house and water poured into the cellar, flooding it to a depth of several feet. After the war the cases, boxes, clocks and furniture contained in it were found disintegrated and reduced to a mass of rotting fragments floating on the water.

Outside the front door was a gravelled square, shut in by the house, the wall of the stable yard to the west and the brewhouse to the north. The last was still in use for household brewing when I was a child and was then a damp ill-lighted outhouse, entered from the yard. An inside stair led up to a mighty vat and the implements used in brewing stood about the floor. The butler, William Woadden, was the last of the master brewers and his expert methods turned out excellent beer. Each of the indoor servants had a quart, as far as I remember, of home-brew at the principal meals of the day and, when beer *was* beer, the allowance must have helped to build up healthy constitutions in the younger members of the household. Good wheaten bread, home-baked, without adulteration, and cheese to go with it were practically unlimited, with plenty of English meat and home-cured bacon.

When William Woadden went into retirement the brewing came to an end. The art, like many another country industry, was killed by the rapid spread of mass-produced commodities.

My father turned the brewhouse into a cheerful garden room. He closed the doorway to the yard and made an entrance facing south, flanked by a wide, stone-mullioned window, with two more windows to the east. The greater part of one wall was occupied by an open hearth and chimney-place of Portland stone, made to burn outsize logs and branches.

This room was a perfect setting for our Christmas trees as well as for small parish teas and meetings, childrens' treats and servants' parties and dances.

It was here that, for several Christmasses, the Lulworth mummers staged their traditional play whose words were carefully guarded, never written down but handed on by word of mouth from one generation to the next. The cast consisted of eight stalwart men, six of them dressed in snow-white linen suits adorned with brightly-coloured bits of glass and tinsel which flashed and glittered in the firelight. Armed with sham swords and wearing towering head dresses like bishops' mitres they were an awe-inspiring sight for infant eyes. Two other members of the company fulfilled the roles of Doctor, Horse and Father Christmas. We watched them, fascinated, as they stamped and swaggered round the floor, declaiming the traditional verse in the good old Dorset tongue.

The brewhouse stored the garden chairs, my sister's incubator and the bicycle which was the apple of my eye. It had remained a dream for many years, the longing to have a bicycle of my own having taken possession of me at the age of nine or ten. Our weekly pocket money stood at threepence until we reached our teens and then advanced to sixpence where it froze until we left them. My father paid our travelling expenses and my mother bought our clothes, but Christmas and birthday presents and other similar outgoings made their claims on our allowances. So that it took a long while to amass the necessary sum and I was nearly twenty when at last the bicycle became my own. Like many another object long desired it proved a disappointment, for rough road surfaces, steep gradients, strong head winds and frequent gates made Tyneham an unsuitable place for cycling for pleasure.

I bought the second-hand machine with all accessories for less than five pounds cash, and it must have been a good one for it was still in good condition when I parted with it after thirty-one years.

Outside the brewhouse, in the lawn, stood an azarool thorn. The tree I knew in my youth was very old and a glorious spectacle it was with its load of peach-like berries in the autumn. It gradually encroached upon the drive and finally had to be sacrified to make more turning space for cars. A young successor took its place and was doing well in 1943, but azarools are very slow in growth. A young tree grown from a Tyneham cutting went with me to Weybridge, moved to Windsor and eventually to Stock and is still, though over fifty years of age, barely six feet high. The berries were a great attraction to the missel-thrushes and they stripped the tree too quickly, though azarool fruit is full of woody seeds and is dry and woolly to the tongue.

The "battered" base of the gable, under the library window, was inhabited by a fascinating colony of self-sown mosses, ferns and flowers. Dwarfed harts' tongues, lady ferns and polypodies, wall rue, ceterach and spleenwort—black and green—found foothold in the crevices between the stones, and there were tufts and clumps of creeping Jenny, mother of thousands, pennywort, sandwort, bittercress, white and yellow stonecrop, pearlwort and pellitory-of-the-wall. But the most cherished denizens of this miniature garden were the tiny yews and hollies which, with a minimum of sustenance and anchorage, braved winter gales and summer thirsts through many human generations.

The stable yard was cobbled with white stone setts over half its area and a wide stone gutter, where the cobbles ceased, took off the water from the carriage washings. Southward the coachhouse stood with its back to the kennel yard, companioned by the saddleroom and stable buildings under one stone-tiled roof. The coachhouse in our day was occupied by a light station brougham, its coachwork painted darkest green and finished with the family crest in its heraldic colours on the doors, a two-wheeled dog-cart, later superseded by a four-wheeled dog-cart having interchangeable shafts and pole, and a low-hung two-wheeled donkey-cart. This little cart was specially built for Uncle John in his old age and was like a shallow dog-cart, beautifully sprung and comfortable to drive in but too heavy for such hilly country.

The two-wheeled trap had figured in an accident while Sydney Mills was coachman. Driving from Wareham in a snowstorm Sydney lost the road on the top of the hill and the frightened horse got out of control. The dog-cart overturned, throwing the old man clear, and horse and trap rolled over and over down the steep declivity. The horse escaped, astonishingly, with one small cut, but the cart was smashed and Sydney's nerve so shaken that he would not drive again. He had a splendid mane of stiff white hair encouraged to stand out in a bush below his livery hat, and as children we firmly believed that, like royal and Lord Mayor's coachmen, he wore a wig.

The brougham's stand in the coachhouse had tackle slung above it for lowering and raising the luggage tray fitting the roof of the great-uncles' carriage. Our own much smaller brougham had a railing round the top in place of the old-fashioned basket. A semi-circular wicker wheel guard, made to keep mud from women's dresses as they climbed in and out of the dog-cart, hung on the wall, and a powerful jack for raising the carriage wheels stood with the clogged thigh-boots for the coachman's wear when washing the carriage.

A good fire burned in the harness-room all the year round on an open brick hearth. A corn-bin stood under the window and its lid made a useful table. All round the wainscoted walls hung harness and saddlery smelling of polish and saddle soap. Carriage whips stood in a row of clips on a special bracket, their pipe-clayed thongs and brightly coloured "flies" secured to the slender bamboo butts. Each saddle had its bridle hung beneath it and the buckles and bosses on the saddlery and black patent leather harness shone like little suns. Our donkey's set of harness and the old pilch saddle with a bucket-stirrup, on which we had our earliest riding lessons, hung by the door, We harnessed the donkey for ourselves when we wanted the cart. Arranged in a circle over the fireplace were the hooks for the button stick, a knuckle-bone for polishing top-boots, a square of chains for cleaning bits and a hare's foot for the finishing of the leathers. A box of silver sand for scouring steel, the sponges, soft soap, polishes and hoof-oils stood on a chest-of-drawers beside the fire, all adding to the saddle-room's wholesome smell. An upright ladder on the stable wall outside the door gave access to the loft whence hay was dropped through trap doors into the barred hayracks in the stalls and boxes. Up in the tallat under the roof the stable cats, a hardy race of gingers, flourished for many years, at war with the household pets.

A pathway from the yard wound past the ferretry and through the shrubbery beyond it to the grindstone, then up some steps to where the meat-safe sheltered in the laurels. The safe was a big square cage of perforated zinc in a wooden frame, well roofed and raised on stout wooden legs. A kitchen messenger could often be seen flitting between kitchen-yard and safe, which furnished a good excuse for brief escapes into the open air.

Passing between the coachhouse and the west wing of the house we come to the dog-yard, sheltered on all four sides by ranges of buildings. Coal and oil stores bounded it to the west, abutting on a flight of steps leading out to the Stable Plot. The stairway faced a wall and the exit lay at a right angle to the steps, so that the yard was perfectly protected from the prevailing winds. Then came the carthouse, built on the level of the Plot and therefore, like the Old House, raised on a grass-topped platform four or five feet high. The wood-house, Old House and the House itself completed the enclosure. An arm of the yard between the Old House and the kitchen wing led to the back door and the entrances to fuel and boiler rooms.

The Old House, once the home of Russells and Chekes and probably dating from the 14th century—though at least one expert put it quite a century earlier—had at some time in the past been turned into a dwelling for the dairyman. George Richards, in his nineties when he died at the beginning of the present century, believed that he was born there. The Russell ownership of Tyneham is not the first to be recorded, for Domesday Book attests that part of the land was held by Robert, Earl of Morton, half-brother of the Conqueror. Later it seems that Tyneham became Bardolfe property. The Harleian MS asserts that "Thomas Bardolfe gave the manner of Estynham to Walter* Russell in free marriage with his daughter Rosye", and so began the Russell tenure, lasting some hundred and fifty years. Rohesia or "Rosye" was the widow of one Henry de la Pomerai of Berry Pomeroy in Devon and, curiously enough, a daughter of this ancient house became, six centuries later, my paternal grandmother. The Russell name died out at Tyneham towards the fourteenth century, when the property passed to four coheiresses, bearing the well-known Dorset names of Chick, Chyke or Cheke, Meere, Fry and Burdon. Most of the Russell property in Tyneham appears to have come eventually to the eldest of the sisters, Joanna Chyke, and continued in that name for several generations, the family regularly sending representatives to Parliament for the borough of Wareham. It was most probably the last of the Chykes who sold it to John Williams of Herringston in 1523 and, from thence onwards, it never again changed hands but passed through male and female lines to the ending of the ownership in 1952.

The original Russell homestead was a hall two storeys high, with an open timber roof of fine design and workmanship. This roof, long hidden by plaster, had been uncovered when I knew it first and still is to be seen in the upper room on the right hand of the stair head. The floors, however, of this chamber and of the one beyond were in a dangerous condition of decay. The rooms were used for lumber, storing onions, garden nets, etc. and, by the cats, as nurseries, where families could be kept from public view and brought up free from interference.

The room on the left at the top of the worn and winding stair was in a sounder state and used as an apple loft and potato store.

A small dark vault whose door was opposite the Tudor entrance served as beer cellar. The butler kept the key, dispensing mugs of beer to such as came on business to the kitchen yard.

* Walter is here a mistake for John.

In the old hall the massive open fireplace, once in the early building on the site of the new south wing, took up the greater part of the inner wall, and its brick oven, still intact, was used for weekly bakings well into the twentieth century. The odd man heated it with faggots of dry furze, and how delectable the golden crusty loaves both looked and smelt when newly baked and carried steaming hot on wooden trays across the yard. The batches lasted the whole household for a week and kept their appetising freshness to the end.

The dairy formed the west end of the Old House buildings on the lower floor. It was reached by a stone-flagged path along the terrace raised above the yard. After the house cows had been sold and when the farm supplied the house with milk this cool and airy room was chiefly used for hanging game and poultry.

It is impossible to think of yards and outhouses without remembering the men whose work lay chiefly in and about them. Except for one short interval the office of odd man was filled, within the compass of my memory, by two men only, both named Charles. Charles I had worked at Tyneham for a long while prior to the death of Uncle John. He was a slow and ponderous old man and hard of hearing. We liked him on account of his indulgence of our mania for riding on 'his' horse and because he took us in the "putt", or two-wheeled cart, on his faggot-hauling expeditions. He "suffered with his feet" and gladly let us fetch the horse from grass for him, though grumbling that we rode his charge too fast. We always hoped old "Punch" would be at the furthest end of the avenue when we went in search of him before our breakfast, so that the homeward ride might last as long as possible. We learned to clamber up the dizzy height of "Punch's" sixteen hands with the help of walls or railings, my younger sister sitting up behind me and clinging to my waist. We trotted, dislocatingly but soberly, to the Cowleaze gate and walked sedately down the lane behind the garden to the Stable plot where (this was the high light of the whole proceeding) our mount took charge and broke into a lumbering gallop, keeping it up until we reached the top of the plot. There he suddenly stopped dead, wheeled round and walked back to his stable door, with a conscious air of having done his best to amuse the children.

One of the odd man's duties was to drive the little waggon to Wareham station to fetch back luggage and now and then old Charles' partiality for beer proved his and a visitor's undoing. Impatient guests, unable to change for dinner, or weary nurses waiting for the wherewithal to make their tired and fretful charges ready for bed, might fume in vain while the hours dragged on without a sign of the returning wanderer. The normal timing for the single journey was about two hours, and guests were warned beforehand of the need to bring essentials with them in a handbag.

Our Charles the Second was beloved Charlie Meech who stayed with the family for over forty years. His mother's second husband, William Taylor, was the Tyneham woodman and Mrs. Taylor ran the

35

laundry with the help of her two daughters, who succeeded to her office when she died. Charlie began as bailiff's horseman at the farm, removing to the House when the farm was let. He rapidly became an institution and indispensable, endearing himself to staff and family alike. Invariably cheerful and ungrudging of his time and trouble, he soon identified himself with all our interests and entered into them with sympathy and zest. In any quandary or troublesome situation the cry increasingly became: "Ask Charlie". He seldom failed to find the right solution to the problem.

In 1943, when houses had to be provided for the exiled Tyneham people, the Taylor family were found a home at Corfe, where for three years my brother and his wife were also housed. Charlie stayed on with them and turned his hand to any necessary task, indoors or out. He lavished his affection on the two 'odd' horses, "Palmer" and his successor "Joan", the last of whom he tended lovingly for over seventeen years. He and his charges talked together as they worked and Charlie grieved for his companion when Joan was pensioned off at the evacuation and sent to grass at Grange.

Charlie was sympathetic with the young, who took to him instinctively. They loved his jokes and most infectious laugh and children staying at Tyneham always asked permission to "go out with Charlie". Long may he live to be a comfort to his friends and set them an example of straightforward, conscientious and unselfish living.

The carthouse held the little waggon, putt and garden ladders. Its dim green twilight, flickering with the motion of the overshadowing trees, intensified our make-believe that the waggon was a ship. Many a stirring voyage in uncharted seas we made in it on rainy days when the wind sang over the roof tops. My father built the granary on brick supports at the top of the plot above the rick stands, little foreseeing that the contents of the library would be housed in it so soon after his death.

The pigstyes, uninhabited as long as I remember, stood back against the wall of the Rookery Wood. Here we kept snails in boxes full of bran and fattened them on lettuce leaves until they were plump and succulent enough to fry over a wood fire in the Museum kitchen.

The last of the buildings in the stable plot was the cowhouse, later turned into a carpenter's shop, with the 'odd horse' stable at one end, the whole stone-tiled and thickly crowned with polypody ferns.

Behind the cowhouse yawned the sawpit, where the bars and gate posts needed on the estate were cut out with a double-handed saw. The gates for the estate were made here, too, fashioned from local timber by a local craftsman, to fit their setting and endure for many years. The rhythmic sighing of the blade drawn down through the wood was one of the many peaceful sounds of Tyneham. The sawpit made a splendid exercising ground for our ferrets. They revelled in the deep sawdust, working themselves to such a pitch of playfulness that going down the rickety ladder to retrieve them became fraught with horrifying possibilities. We used to dare our innocent and unsuspecting female cousins—charming little creatures that we were—to go into the pit and catch the ferrets for us, knowing full well that our excited pets would have climbed their stockings long before they reached the foot of the ladder.

A metalled pathway from the House led through an iron wicket to the Rookery Wood and crossed it to the private road to Worbarrow.

The whole of the Stable plot was grassed and made a pleasant playground for the fowls and ducks who had the run of it. The ravens never troubled the poultry yard and Tyneham, happily, was free from carrion crows, but jackdaws kept a sharp look-out for unguarded chicks, and rats were an ever-present menace. Foxes came down from the cliffs at night. In recent years rogue badgers took to making onslaughts on the fowl houses, digging to undermine them and attacking doors with their powerful claws.

A fern-leafed beech of my father's planting occupied a triangle of turf at the foot of the back drive, and an old, prolific walnut-tree stood at the western limit of the plot. Its crop was usually raided by the rooks before the nuts were ripe enough to fall. The tang of the bruised leaves after autumn gales was like those river smells beloved of Rupert Brooke ". . . thrilling sweet and rotten, Unforgettable, unforgotten".

A couple of great sycamores and an ash threw shade across the entrance to the Stable yard. Beyond them stacks of timber waiting to be sawn leaned up against the walls of the manure pound. There was no need of artificial fertilisers then and, save for aphis in the hothouses, no pests requiring chemical insecticides attacked the crops. The yield of vegetable produce did not fail, and its consumers throve upon it.

CHAPTER IV

The Garden

FROM the main entrance, looking north, the eye fell first on the shrubberies and trees on either side of the Little Avenue or Gap, a vista also known as "William Woadden's Avenue", which owed its origin to the old butler. During an illness of great-uncle John, William suggested that some trees be felled to give the invalid a view across the valley to the hill. Later the Gap was cleared of shrubs and grassed down by my father. My mother planted it with hundreds of narcissi, a joy to look at in the spring. On the eastward side the trees were widely spaced and in the mossy turf between them strawberries and violets, primroses and cyclamen, anemones, dogs tooth violets, periwinkles and a host of other little flowers made up a pattern as gay as any that decks the Heavenly floors of Fra Angelico.

Beyond, where the ground rose steeply to the kitchen garden wall, my father cut a new path through a grove of rhododendrons and planted flowering trees and shrubs in this warm and favoured corner. I can remember garrya elliptica and rhododendron praecox, callicarpa, calycanthus, wych hazel and pecan trees, snowy mespilus, Benthamia and escallonia. A fan palm—*chaemoerops fortuneii*—braved the gales for many years and grew to an imposing height, only to be beheaded by the W.A.A.F's who occupied the House, to make a party decoration for their Mess. In 1950 it was putting out new growth. The best of all the rhododendrons by this walk was the vivid scarlet Smithii, flowering early in the spring before the trees had opened any leaves. Its blaze of colour faced the beautifully shaped horse chestnut at the edge of the lawn, a happy planting by my Biggs great-grandmother when she came to live at Tyneham early in the nineteenth century. Her precious gift to her descendants was the first to spread its pale green fingers every year and often showed a leaf as early as the first or second week in February. To me it was an annual delight to find the little crinkled leaflet pressed in a Tyneham letter, letting me know that spring in the favoured valley had begun. The chestnut's lower branches dipped and rested on the grass, making a high green-shaded secret room for us to play in.

Between the rhododendrons and the chestnut tree a path wound up the slope to the kitchen garden door, kept locked, in common with all other garden entrances except when gardeners were working, in the great-uncle's time. Beyond the door a steep ascent led up to the highest level of the garden, accompanied by a bright herbaceous border. This

38

first walled area was intersected by straight gravel paths edged with stone tiles or miniature box hedges. A border ran from east to west below the twelve foot wall at the top and in this sheltered spot there flourished lemon verbena, belladonna lilies, 'lobster claw'* English wild tulips, clerodendron, crinum, allspice, crinodendron Hookeri, aralia, choisya, campanula glomerata and a carpeting of the lovely canary yellow tropoeolum polyphyllum, backed by wistaria, a fig tree and a peach.

The cage for bush fruit occupied the south-west corner of the garden, a pound with doors at either end and plenty of room for moving freely between rows and bushes. The gooseberries had pride of place and they rejoiced in the soil and climate. I cannot remember a year in which they failed to produce a heavy crop, so heavy in some seasons that we could not cope with it. There were a number of varieties, the greater part of them unnamed and probably their names had long disappeared from growers' lists. The one kind happily unrepresented was the big, smooth, watery and tasteless fruit which swamps the market now, a very poor relation of the older sorts for which one seeks in vain. The Tyneham "coppersmiths" were small, dark, almost hairless berries, not much larger than a prize black currant but sweet and full of flavour. There were others just as luscious ; a large crimson fruit ; round, hairy golden ones ; smooth, oval berries, yellow, red and green ; bright red ones with a clean, sharp taste, a pale transparent green variety, red-speckled—each with its own delicious, easily distinguishable flavour. In the gooseberry season we were allowed to raid the bushes twice a day but were limited to twenty gooseberries at a time.

Beyond the gooseberries the currant grove began, red, white and black, and then the lines of raspberry canes, bearing a crop which never disappointed though liable to mildew in wet seasons.

Asparagus and strawberries and peas, both green and sweet, accounted for the space remaining in this wholly walled-in garden. Espalier pears and apples bordered the paths and fruit trees—peaches, greengages, nectarines and plums—covered the walls of local stone. The hothouses monopolised a stretch of the high north wall, the first reserved for flowers, supplying the House, the church, and village funerals and weddings. The second hothouse contained the vines, long shelves of arum lilies for the altar, and staging to accommodate, first seedling boxes and then, later in the season, ripening nectarines and peaches, figs and pears.

Close to the greenhouses and in the angle of the north and east walls the violet frames were snugly sheltered, sharing their sunny corner with a big carnation bed and the stone-lined tank of clear spring water which supplied the garden. The water hawthorn growing in the tank was seldom without a sprinkling of sweet-scented flowers afloat

* Clianthus punicius.

upon the water. Fat gold fish, brought as infants from the Fair at Wood-
bury Hill, swam lazily between the leaves. This sun-warmed corner was
a place to linger in on fine days in midwinter. Its high walls shielded a
catawba vine, bignonia, myrtle, diplacus and the famous orange-tree.
The tree was covered by a glass light in the winter months and, in
exceptional cold, by a layer of sacking. Otherwise unprotected it bore
fruit whose quantity and degree of ripeness varied with the season. It
had been known to ripen as many as two hundred oranges in a favourable summer. It came to an untimely end while still in its prime through
having its roots attacked and gnawed by mice. Another tree was planted
in its place but had not begun to bear by 1943.

A few more things that I can remember growing in this section of
the garden are the bloodroot sent us by a "cousin" of our name in
Ohio, snowy blossoms which appeared before the leaves and, in their
bud stage, looked like pigeon's eggs ; some wood lilies or trilliums
from the same kind giver and his baneberry or "dolls' eyes", loquats
and the "York and Lancaster" roses bordering the middle path.

A self-sown garden flourished on the old stone walls, where crevices
gave root-hold to all kinds of ferns and flowers, amongst them toad-
flax, linum, Cheddar pink, snapdragon, wallflower, valerian and
Canterbury bell.

The warm enclosure was a paradise for butterflies and they thronged
the sun-drenched borders. White admirals grew common in the later
years, and painted ladies, peacocks, commas, tortoiseshells, small
coppers and red admirals crowded the megasea blooms and basked on
the sunny stones. A Camberwell beauty, captured by my mother, was
immortalised by Martin Travers in the beautiful east window he made
for Tyneham church in memory of Mrs. Draper. I found a dead and
battered long-tailed blue, the first, I think, to be recorded for the
county, amongst some fallen leaves in the Coppice Walk after a summer
gale. Though not particularly rich in woodland butterflies the hills and
cliffs encouraged quantities of chalk lovers :—Clifton, holly, small and
chalkhill blues, brown argus, skippers, graylings, meadow browns and
gatekeepers, small heaths, walls, small and green-veined whites,
fritillaries and clouded yellows. Along the cliff top marbled whites
abounded, as did the sluggish burnet moths, clinging in hundreds to
the bents in all their splendour of metallic green and crimson.

An archway in the wall between the two walled gardens held a
wrought iron gate of light and elegant design, later to suffer sadly at
the feet of W.A.A.F's and soldiers climbing the wall into the garden
when it was out of bounds.

The second garden was for fruit and vegetables only and kept the
house supplied throughout the year. Peaches and nectarines were
trained against the walls with a few pears and plums. An ancient
Jargonelle pear produced a heavy crop in favourable years and other-
well-tried kinds with no objection to the clayey soil were Doyenne du
Comice and Beurre d'Amanlis. The plums included golden gages and

Coe's Golden Drop. In schoolroom days we manufactured muslin bags for figs and peaches, so that the fruit could ripen safe from wasps and birds. Long narrow runners, netted in winter evenings by the two great-uncles, still caught nectarines and peaches if they fell.

Cherry trees and melon frames were sited north of the garden wall in a narrow strip of ground containing tool and potting-sheds and hot-house furnace. A quickset hedge, dividing it from the lane, was set on a high grass bank, and here appeared the earliest signs of spring— pale brimstone butterflies and sluggish oil beetles, the first bright celandines and sweet white violets.

An ice-cold spring came bubbling up in a tiny spring house at the end of this back garden and until fairly recent years provided drinking water for the House. The footmen fetched the water from it in big earthen pitchers.

The north-east angle of the second garden enclosed a garden seat, placed at the junction of two walks, sheltered by high walls from the north and east and looking back towards the House. This pleasant corner and the upper path which it commanded were the objective of first walks after family illnesses, and what a joy it was to rest in the scented air and see the avenue trees and Great Wood from above once more. Virginian creeper clothed the wall behind the bench and har-boured tribes of snails. Extracting them from between its twisted stems and from the crannies of the wall provided gentle recreation for the convalescent.

The herb garden came last of the enclosures. Here grew the arti-chokes, horse radishes and pot herbs, thyme, sage, marjoram, basil, fennel, chives, mint, tarragon and other savoury smelling things.

The whole of the kitchen garden was most happily situated on a hillside lying open to the south, protected from north and east and, to a certain extent, from the prevailing wind (though, even so, with all the screens of wall and hedge, the cabbages were often socketed or blown out of the ground unless secured to stakes, in the winter months). No wonder that subtropical and tender plants and shrubs survived and flourished in their sheltered quarters. Spring flowers appeared some weeks before they opened in the inland gardens, though trees, as a whole, were late in coming into leaf, and early daffodils and tulips made a fair display. The tulips in the first walled garden turned the pathways into avenues of brilliant colour. The garden was opened to the public, every May, to show the tulips and the bluebells in the wood, and later in the summer when the flower garden round the house was at its best.

A gate at the south-west corner of the second garden led into the Fig Walk where azalea bushes grew among the grass. A glorious scarlet-flowered bush was the most conspicuous. This dazzling variety is no longer to be found in catalogues and none that I have seen in other gardens, with the exception of an unnamed bush at Wisley, have rivalled it for brilliancy of colour and prolific blooming. Sprays of its vivid, flamelike flowers above the altar of the village church, ablaze in the early morning sun at Whitsuntide, were a sight not easily forgotten.

Old fig trees under the garden wall were neighboured by a medlar whose brown and woolly-tasting fruit produced delicious jelly, smooth and translucent, ruby red and sweet, a delicacy for dessert the whole year round. Medlar and figs were shielded from the south-west wind by a screen of clipped yew hedge. Beyond it lay the rhododendron border, triumphing over difficult conditions, for all the stiff clay soil had been removed and replaced by peat from Povington. Camellias and a gingko shared the border with the rhododendrons.

Until the years between the wars three gardeners were employed and kept well occupied. Two were needed for the mowing-machine, one pushing and one pulling, and all the slopes and terraces were mown by hand. To present-day minds it must appear fantastic that so many people were required for the maintenance of so small a place as Tyneham. They might be surprised at the proportion of my father's income which, even in days of lower wage rates, went in wages. The money could have been employed in other far more satisfying ways but he and his like were still old-fashioned in their view of their responsibilities. To him the place he had inherited was a trust, a piece of England to be kept intact, unspoilt and handed on in at least as good a state as that in which it came to him, and the primary charge upon his means was the employment of the families on his estate. It might be thought that he had no need of so many dependents but, rightly or wrongly, he believed that they were in need of him. Whether their occupations are to be considered productive must depend on the assessor's individual scale of values and on what he holds to be the ultimate aim of life. To one accustomed from his childhood to the centralising, mass-directing policies of the brave new world, the whole conception of exclusive inter-dependence in a small community must be barely comprehensible. I merely state that such things did exist and were the normal principle of rural life. On large estates the system was more thoroughly developed, but even the smaller properties conformed to it. Income derived from the estate went back to the estate, in wages, maintenance and where it was possible, improvements. With almost all the landowners I knew there was no question of its being otherwise. The men who held the land in trust believed that to preserve the land and its traditions was, in the long run, best for the land and for all concerned with it. A sudden appearance of prosperity among the agricultural workers, following on the war, may seem to contradict this view, but history works slowly and the final verdict is not yet.

When we were young we were inclined to grumble, now and then, at the lack of means for holidays or treats and at the small economies imposed upon us. To take a few examples :—we were not allowed to use a public vehicle whenever it was possible to walk, and meals in restaurants were out of order if a packet of food could be supplied from home. Amusements costing money were severely rationed and very little was spent on toys or playthings. The family finances often reached a state of crisis and various methods of retrenchment were discussed, but never a possible economising at the expense of servants present or past. A large proportion of the cottages at Grange were occupied by pensioners, happy to keep their homes about them to the last. My father housed old people at a purely nominal rent, often unpaid for years and finally wiped off the slate. In later years when Worbarrow was "discovered" by the outside world, the houses there would have let to summer tenants for fantastic sums, but the old folks' right to stay on in their homes was held to be as sacred as our own.

No doubt there were bad landlords, here and there, but I am convinced that they were the exceptions. One such in the county, with a name for ruthless treatment of his tenants, was shunned and execrated for his conduct by his fellow squires, which would appear to mark him out as a departure from the normal.

James Curtis was head gardener, an expert at his work and a trusted friend, for eighteen years and was succeeded by his second in command, Tom Gould, who worked in the garden at Tyneham for more than forty years. Tom was a cousin of the south Tyneham Everitts and married their daughter, Virtue. He served in the Dorset Regiment and fought at Chitral. In 1914 he was recalled and served all through the first World War. In the latter part of it he was employed as guide to parties going up to the firing line, for his exceptional memory and perfect sense of direction never failed him in the darkest night and in the labyrinth of the trenches. Exposure to the terrible conditons of trench warfare undermined his health, though he continued at his cherished occupation until the sore disaster of evacuation struck the valley. The second war reduced his garden staff and he was often single handed. No stranger could have guessed it from the perfect trim in which he kept the garden. His only training had been in the subordinate tasks of a second gardener but on promotion he immediately gave evidence of skill and knowledge in all branches of his work. When middle-aged he chose, with characteristic moral courage and humility, to be confirmed and thenceforth was a faithful churchgoer and communicant, succeeding William Taylor in the post of parish clerk and sexton. Tom had a splendid head, with strong and clear-cut features full of character, and would have made the perfect model for a militant saint. Towards the end of his life he must have qualified for sainthood, bedridden as he was for many years and bearing his long, slow martyrdom with uncomplaining patience. He felt my father's death acutely and told me with tears that he and the old master had never had a difference or "words" in all their years together, a tribute to his own integrity as well as to the value put upon it by my father.

The outpost limes of the avenue stood on the lawn, and here the earliest snowdrops opened in the pockets of plushy moss between the spreading roots of the old trees.

The lawn was separated from the avenue by a deep sunk fence and stone-lined ditch, dry in the summer droughts. It carried the surface water from the Wood and Avenue and, after heavy rain, a brawling torrent poured across it from one square culvert to another at the opposite end. There the flood water disappeared to plunge below the lawn and was no more seen until it re-emerged as a lively stream in the Rookery Wood. We had some anxious times when dogs chased rabbits into the drain and, just before the first World War, my father enlarged the culverts, closing their entrances with hinged iron grids. Two urns of Swanage stone, copied from those in the park at Grange, were placed on plinths at either end of the haha at this time.

The lawn formed part of the valley's central floor and marked the meeting place between the limestone and the wealden clay, an interesting foundation for a garden, affording scope for growing trees and plants of great variety. In front of the house the grass gave way to a terrace of large square flagstones, furnished with garden chairs and benches. One of my happiest mental pictures of my father shows him sitting there in deep contentment on calm summer evenings, watching the shadow of the house creep slowly over the lawn, his field-glasses at hand all ready to be focused on a passing bird or on a distant figure like a tiny chessman moving, dark against the sky, across the opening at the top of the Avenue. He loved to watch the peregrines and ravens homing to the cliff and took a special pleasure in the calling of the ring doves in the lime trees as the sun went down.

A double rank of pots full of red geraniums glowed scarlet against the background of grey stone, attracting humming-bird hawk moths and the great green grasshoppers which, I am told, are still to be seen and heard at Tyneham

Round the south corner of the house an old magnolia faced the sun, trained up the gable end but long since self-supporting, accompanied by winter jessamine and a cardinal-red cydonia. The whole of the south wing was over-run by a cream-coloured Banksia rose brought back from Oxford by great-uncle John some hundred and thirty years ago. A path along the back of the Old House curved up the slope to the terraces through sycamores and beeches. Under the trees the ground in spring was thick with snowdrops, aconites and crocuses. Snowdrops had spread along the steep embankment of the upper terrace and covered the rise to the gate of the Rookery Wood.

A tilted pattern of flower beds broke the expanse of shaven grass between the lawn and upper terrace, tall Riccartonii fuchsias completing the design. After the building of the Hole Field reservoir my father made a circular basin, rimmed, lined and stepped with stone, in the level ground between the Terraces to take the overflow. It soon became the home of newts, or "evvets", and water boatmen and a host of smaller fry. My brother added a fountain made by himself, whose gentle splashing emphasized the quiet of summer nights.

A line of yuccas marked the top of the upper terrace's almost vertical embankment. They were a handsome sight when carrying their creamy, scented spikes of thickly clustered bells. The weight of the top-heavy heads soon grew too much for the brittle stems and every year a few were snapped off by the wind. The roots sent up fresh growth to flower again in two or three years' time. The specimen field maple growing in the bank was a perfectly shaped tree and the largest I have seen.

One of the most enchanting views of the house could be had from the east end of the upper terrace and there were many charming pictures of it taken from this point, whence all the lovely colouring of the roof tiles was well seen. The Purbeck ashlar of the front had weathered to a soft warm grey and it was further mellowed by its patina of many-coloured lichens. These, in all possible shades of primrose, orange, silver, ochre, rust and Indian red, patterned the surface of the stone, whose aspect changed continually according to the season, day and hour. In rainy weather I have seen it looking slaty blue while, after a hot, dry spell, the stone would bleach to palest shades of cinnamon, buff and ash. The morning sunshine flooded it with gold and on cloudy days its colour ranged from cool blue-grey through shades of lavender and lilac. The eaves and window sills, the porch and string courses threw deep-toned shadows on the surface of the stone. This harmony of colour and the clean lines of roof and gables stood out clear from the background of tall trees and distant hill, a triumph of masterly design and right material in a perfect setting.

My brother, in a paper on the house, described it happily as "quiet and unpretentious, owing its charm to its restful proportions and to the lovely patina that 350 years have given to the local Purbeck stone. The whole composition is graceful and avoids the pompousness of many of the classical revivals, which would be quite out of place in these secluded rural surroundings".

This was the home which sheltered our young days and was the keynote of our whole existence.

CHAPTER V

Out and About

FREED from the schoolroom as the clock struck twelve we made for the open air, whatever the weather might be, and were off in search of my father who must be somewhere about the farm. Our first objective usually was the high ground on the Cowleaze Knap, a good spot for a reconnaissance. Over the tree tops of the Rookery Wood and Gwyle the whole of the South Hill, from the West Plantation to the Bay, lay open to our view. Eastwards the Upper Horse Close, Nine Acres and the Quarry Field were visible above the near ridge of the Knap. To the north both Limekiln Fields, North Hill itself and the pastures at its foot were quickly scanned, and down the valley lay the village roofs with Baltington beyond, the whole entrancing picture backed by Flower's Barrow, Bindon Hill, and, on the far horizon, Portland, lying athwart the twelve mile stretch of sea.

This perfect scene would often draw us out, in later years, to climb the Knap on summer evenings and watch the last light fading from the valley, then from the hills, while still reflected in the glassy sea, until it became "a width, a shining peace, under the night". Sometimes the moon crept up the sky behind us while we watched and waited there and, turning towards home, we found its light competing with the dusky fires smouldering in the west. (The harvest moon rose in the opening of the avenue and we watched, each autumn, for the great gold disc to show its rim over Shoemaker's Lane and gradually fill up the space between the arching trees.)

The two contrasting scents which met us in those strolls remain embedded in my memory—the warm, sweet smell of sunburnt grass, unlike the smell of any grass in inland places, and the sudden waft of fresh, damp air, laden with cool, green fragrances of moss and fern, inside the entrance gate. However hot the weather, sunset at Tyneham always brought refreshment in the light breeze stirring off the sea and the cool breathings from the woods.

A clump of trees, now gone, Scots pines and hawthorns, on the slope to the west of the approach, figured in many photographs of Worbarrow Bay and Portland taken from the Knap. On the opposite side of the road a characteristically wind-swept thorn-tree, bent over until parallel with the ground, attracted the photographers and made a plaything for the young of many generations. It was hacked down for firewood by the "army of occupation". My sister-in-law, who heard

46

the sound of the axe and ran to save the venerable tree, came just too late and found it fallen.

The old approach to the House once crossed the Knap to the east of the present road and the line of its more direct and steeper course could still be traced. Below it the "New Forest", planted by great-uncle John, a strip of mixed deciduous trees and firs, protected the walled garden from the northerly winds. Between this belt and the garden lay a gated lane, the home of wild white strawberries, nettle-leaved campanula and meadow cranesbill. The woodmen, by my father's orders, spared the wild flowers when they trimmed the banks, keeping the beauty of the self-sown gardens.

I have strayed some distance from the top of the Knap and must return to our inspection of the valley. We seldom failed to track my father down without delay and spent the remainder of the morning happily in his always interesting and stimulating company. He noticed everything he passed, expecting us to do the same, and showed his pleasure if we called attention to some detail we detected for ourselves.

He was a competent judge of cattle and of the practical side of farming, disliking all untidy, slip-shod ways and quickly roused to wrath by scamping or by rough treatment of an animal or tool. The men, I fancy, stood in awe of his tongue, but knew very well that the bark was fiercer than the bite and that good honest work was sure of his approval. He had a deep appreciation and respect for the conscientious workman and numbered many such among his valued friends.

We picked up plenty of useful knowledge about trees and beasts and farming generally while in his company. The livestock were his special interest and each animal was visited every day, however far from home it might be grazing. If anything prevented him from carrying out his round of inspection we were his deputies, with orders not to be content until we had put up every beast found lying down and satisfied ourselves that it had stretched itself on rising. My father kept a pedigree herd of Devon cattle and showed with some success. The big thick-coated cows did well in the rough conditions under which they lived, though from the dairy point of view their yield was disappointing. My mother introduced some Guernsey heifers to improve the cream, but the six attractive little creatures would not tolerate the stiff, wet soil and came to an untimely end.

The common breed of sheep in Purbeck at that time was the Dorset Horn and my father's introduction of a Shropshire flock was looked upon as a daring innovation. The experiment succeeded in the capable hands of Shepherd Lucas. In spite of gloomy prophecies by the neighbours the imported ewes throve on the hillside pastures and produced a healthy crop of lambs each year. We sometimes had some lambs at the House to rear by hand and found them most engaging in their infant days before they reached the rough and headstrong stage.

The lower levels of the Eweleazes were good pastures, laid up in autumn for the "lamb's grass" in the spring. The upper portions of

47

both fields rose steeply, covered with "rowaty", thorn trees and brakes of gorse, with stunted ashes growing in the sheltered hollows. Above them a dry wall shut off the arable land on the top of the cliff.

The eastern Eweleaze held the spring and reservoir which, except for drinking water in the early days, supplied the House until the Hole Field reservoir was built. The water from the limestone hill was hard and cold and very good to drink, though once, when I lived at Weybridge and was staying at Tyneham, it struck me that it had a peculiar flavour. My father did not relish my remark upon it, retorting that a course of water from the main had evidently spoilt my palate for the genuine article. Later I set out to investigate and, led to the Eweleaze reservoir by a spiciness on the wind, discovered a long dead rabbit floating in the water. The cart-horses at grass had broken part of the door and left an opening wide enough to admit a thirsty rabbit. It is fair to say that nobody was one whit the worse for drinking the gamey broth.

Our progress with my father was a leisurely one, with frequent stops to examine farm and estate work or to exterminate a weed. He could not bear to pass a thistle by and his score of spudded weeds over many years must have mounted up to millions. He did improve the pastures to a great extent but the wind brought seeds from neighbouring farms with disappointing regularity. I have seen the banks and hedge bottoms white with thistle down on autumn days. The plague of ragwort was unknown on Tyneham property.

In winter time our afternoon hours for lessons were from half-past three to six, with a half-hour break for tea. With lengthening days the times were changed and work was finished before tea, so that the evenings were our own. No "home work" robbed us of the blessed freedom of those outdoor evenings. We often kept my mother company, taking the dogs for exercise. Her favourite walk was to the Egliston boundary, through Fig Walk, Coppice Walk and up Shoemaker's Lane. The Coppice Walk, entered by another Chinese-pattern gate, was a narrow belt of woodland bordering the Avenue. Its tall trees formed the north side of the vista from the house, and under them bamboos and hazel coppice, rhododendrons, ferns and partridge berry covered the ground on either side of the central path. Lent lilies grew in the undergrowth and the top of the walk was carpeted with lesser periwinkles and anemones. In May its whole length was a fragrant sea of bluebells. The Avenue itself was thick with primroses. The village children came up to help us pick them for the church on Good Friday afternoons and filled big baskets in exchange for hot-cross buns. I can remember very few occasions when wet weather interfered with picking, though on Easter Day, so it seems to me, it often rained. The flowers, bunched and disposed in every basin, bucket, jug and bowl that the house could spare, remained in the cool of the Brewhouse until Easter Eve.

Most of the farm men in the valley worked as usual on Good Friday, but Uncle John had made a workless day of it at Tyneham so that the men could attend the morning service. The rest of the day was employed, according to immemorial tradition, in setting their potatoes.

One of the most attractive views of Tyneham House was from the crossing of the Avenue by Shoemaker's Lane. The trees on either side of the Avenue latterly screened too much of the house's front but in great-aunt Mary's sketches the whole of the east facade is visible and the sea can be seen above the chimneys. The unexpected vista never failed to take the stranger by surprise as he came out of the wooded portion of the lane.

From one spot in the Avenue a shout would rouse a plaintive, faraway echo from the walls of the house. It was enchanting, in a silent hour, to call and listen for the faint response, like the voice of a long-departed child of Tyneham speaking across the generations to the child beneath the trees.

Shoemaker's Lane lived up to its name when I knew it first. Its surface was of bulky stones worn smooth by wheels and hooves and there were slippery outcrops of the native rock where winter torrents had washed away the upper layers. My father had the big stones broken up and the top re-dressed which made a tolerable road of it. A bank between the lane and wood was loved by the scarlet fungus known as "jews' ears" or, with more elegance, as "fairies' baths". They glowed against their background of bright emerald moss, inviting us to take them home and keep them in wet moss-filled saucers on our window ledges.

To the left of the lane, between the Upper and Lower Belts, lay the Lower Horse Close. My father furnished it with a large stone cattle shed built in 1899, and further improved the field by planting strips of trees and copsewood at the eastern end as a windbreak for the young stock in their winter quarters. They shared a drinking-place with an enclosing arm or in Dorset speech, a leg, of the Upper Horse Close. The lower Close was long, flat, dull and full of agrimony plants, to be avoided when the seeds were ripe. They clung to passing garments, working their way into the fabric, whence they were only pulled with difficulty and with damage to the stuff.

The lane ran out into the Upper Horse Close and there its stony surface ended in a grassy track across the field through a thicket of thorn and ash to the boundary gate. A few more steps and, from the crest of the hill, the whole expanse of the Channel came into view. Below, South Egliston lay hidden in the trees and to the left the stone-tiled boathouses at Sharnel clustered against the cliff. Then came the curve of Kimmeridge Bay, with dark shale cliffs surmounted by the "folly" of Clavel's Tower, the Kimmeridge cottages strung along the village street and, up the park beyond them, Smedmore's old grey front. The scarp of Swyre Head towered behind them all, and the whole magnificent scene was closed by the rugged outline of Saint Aldhelm's Head. Even in calmest weather the long-drawn line of white-topped water showed where Saint Aldhelm's ever-restless race ran far out into the sea.

49

The good salt air brought scents of sea and shore to the hill, with an oily streak of "Kimmeridge Coal" from the cottage chimneys.

My mother liked to follow the hill top in its switchback course from the boundary back to the summit of Tyneham Cap and thence to the Ocean Seat. The highest point of the Cap, 550 feet above the sea, commanded a further sweep of coast to westward, with West Bay shining beyond the Chesil Beach. Inland the eye was led into blue distances above the dip in the northern ridge at Lawfordshare Gate. Immediately below the Cap, on the landward side, hill pastures slanted down to the edge of the Great Wood, where outpost sycamores and elms leant sideways from the buffetings of the gales. Even on quiet summer days their twisted branches still looked tortured by the wind. These dry and stony hill-top pastures had a carpeting of little snailshells without occupants. I think that for the most part they were either *caperata* or *virgata*. A tradition held that the great Roman snail (*pomatia*) had inhabited the fields but though we searched for them with unquenchable hope it never was rewarded.

The eastern pasture, known as Quarry Field or Calves' House Ground, contained the disused pit whence the stone was hewn for the building of the House. The western, French Grass Ground, derived its name from some long past sowing with lucerne. It bore the marks of ploughing from the time when it was broken up and sown to wheat in the Napoleonic wars.

Another walk my mother chose in favourable weather was to Lawfordshare Gate, sometimes by way of Almsgrove, turning back along the ridge through Maiden's Grave Gate. The name preserved the memory—through how many years?—of some poor suicide, found hung in the Baltington cowstalls and reputed to be buried here, the nearest thing to a cross roads that the parish could afford. A clumsy coffin shape was cut into the bark of the Coffin Tree, a very old oak by the road, near the wood, to commemorate the tragedy.

Almsgrove itself, or Ameswood as the natives called it, hung foursquare on the hillside facing south and was intoxicating with the scent of bluebells in the spring. In summer time the North Hill was aglow with foxgloves, a roseate foreground for the panoramic view of Dorset from the top. The vast heath, set with shining pools like silver coins on a dark expanse of carpet, lay below and from it rose the call of curlews wild as the heath itself, the drumming of snipe above the great bog known as the Earls' Kitchen and, sometimes, the liquid sound of Lulworth's sixteenth century bells.

From the other side of the road the land dropped steeply to the valley where village, farms and fields were backed by the unexpected pie-crust edging of the opposite height. From Lawfordshare Gate a bridle-path, believed by my brother to mark a very ancient track, sloped back across the face of the hill to the top of the Limekiln Plantation where it crossed the boundary fence between the two estates of Grange and Tyneham, joining the Wareham road near North Egliston

Farm. A footpath branching from it, where it left the Tyneham property, passed through the Limekiln wood, a mixed plantation of Scots pine, beech, elm and alder, to which my father added birch and Cornish elms. A pair of long-eared owls frequented the plantation and nested there for many years.

The arable Upper and Lower Limekiln Fields were always good for a covey or two of partridges. I treasure memories of golden evenings in the Lime Kilns after harvest (not, as in these days, half way through the summer, but in September), when the westering sun lit up the tree trunks on the edges of distant plantings, so that each stem glowed bright and cleanly cut against the indigo darkness of the woods ; still, autumn days when each sound was softened and diminished and yet crystal clear. The velvety notes of ring doves calling and replying in the deep of the woods drifted across the valley, small as the oboe part in an orchestra of mice, with brittle, husky voices of the rooks—a very different sound from their springtime chorus—and the clicking call of a partridge, like the tick of a watch.

A deep enchantment of a country of high hills and shut-in valleys, even more satisfying than the extended range over which the eye can travel, is the far distance whence the sounds of rural life can reach the ear, distinct, intact, but so reduced in volume as to seem like echoes of some far, invisible, Lilliput. The children's words could be distinguished as they called to one another in the village street. The microscopic sounds instead of breaking emphasized the enveloping silence, just as some delicate tracery accents the shape and curves of a monotonous surface. The listening ear becomes attuned to the threads and beads of sound until they form an exquisite pattern of music in the mind.

When airs so gentle as to be almost imperceptible were stirring from the east, the "charm" of Kingston bells was sometimes added to the fairy concert, their chime no louder than the tinkling of a musical box.

Below the Limekiln Fields the trees of Long Coppice marched along the stream and, crossing the coppice, we came by Cuckoo Pound to the Cowleaze Knap and so to the garden lane and home.

It often happened that my mother had some errand to a neighbour up or down the valley, at Gaulter Cottages or in the heath at Povington and, when she could not go herself, she sent us with her messages and enquiries, invalid dishes, medicines, books or baby clothing as the case required. We thoroughly enjoyed these expeditions and through them made many dear and lifelong friends. One of the furthest missions was to Kimmeridge, where Shepherd Sansom's crippled daughter, Jessie, could never have enough of "reading" or of talks with someone from outside her sickroom. She gave us through her example of uncomplaining, gentle patience far more than we could ever give to her.

We liked especially to visit Louis Stickland at the sea end of South Egliston Gwyle. The little house was crowded with his handiwork,

51

beautifully finished furniture and model ships. The Sticklands had been fishermen and boatbuilders for generations and bore the reputation of being "able to do anything with their hands". Louis himself, a fine and dignified old man as I remember him, was thoughtful and well read, a talker well worth hearing. His mother had been governess to the Mansel family at Smedmore. He walked to Tyneham church every Sunday morning, in a dark frock coat and square-top hat, whatever the weather, taking the difficult path round Tyneham Cap and striking across to the Farm from the Ocean Seat. It was only on very stormy days that he varied his route and came by Egliston Gwyle, Parson's Mead and Shoemaker's Lane. His faithful attendance at church was matched by old Samuel Morey's from over the opposite hill, whose place in the transept was never unfilled as long as his thin and crooked legs could carry him over from Povington.

Will Stickland, Louis' only son, inherited his father's skill and artistry in joinery and carving. He kept the family tradition alive long after his father's death. The evacuation robbed him of his home, his boats and workshops and he failed to recover from the shock of the uprooting. For a while he stayed on in the Gaulter cottages, then, when it grew too evident that the promises of reinstatement would not be honoured, moved down to Plymouth to be near his sailor son but did not long survive the change.

So ended one more line of English craftsmen whose chief pride was in their handiwork and who enriched their country by their industry and integrity. Dorset could ill afford to lose them.

CHAPTER VI

Worbarrow

IN summer time we bathed at Worbarrow when morning school was done. To snatch up hats and towels and harness up the donkey was the work of a very few moments. "Blitz" always shared our hurry and excitement and hardly gave us time to tumble into the cart before he was off at a gallop, had swung through the gate of the stable yard and had taken us spinning at speed round the Plot. The gate at its end was perennially open so nothing impeded our headlong career till we checked at the gate of the Eweleaze.

My father connected the farm with the Rookery Wood by a length of new road. Before that the way lay across untracked grass, with ridges and slopes to add zest to the gallop.

From farm to bay the road had been constructed by the Admiralty as a means of access to the coastguard station and its gates were of alien pattern, solid and very heavy. Before the existence of the metalled way the track to the sea ran along the top edges of the Corn Grounds inside the wall of Gold Down. It came to be known as the Upper Road and was preferred by walkers but no longer used by wheels.

All the way down from the House to Bay the Lower Road accompanied the Gwyle and followed the bends of the stream, while the Corn Grounds bordered it upon its other side.

At the end of them a path and slippery steps to the right of the road wound down into Fern Hollow. Across the way the cottage known as Tizzard's faced the south. This had at one time been a beerhouse kept by one David Miller with a wooden leg. A lean-to shed against its wall served as stable and carthouse for George Selby, our popular little postman, who brought the mail from Wareham every morning and spent the day at Worbarrow in his allotment or working with the fishermen. In the afternoon he put his pony to and drove back to the village post office to collect the outgoing post. He called at the House soon after eight o'clock each morning and snatched a hasty breakfast.

Our letters still came under lock and key in a leather wallet, though the head of the house no longer opened it and sorted the mail and the butler kept the key. His, too, was the task of opening the last evening's "Globe", crumpled by transit through the post, and ironing it out before it took its place on the Oak Hall table. We wrote requests to the Wareham postmaster and put them with money in the outgoing bag. The stamps and postal orders needed were returned in it next day.

The afternoon post, with the daily newspapers, was left at the post office at Creech, two miles away, and had to be sent for every day. On

Sundays there was an early morning delivery and collection. Outgoing letters on a week day were collected by the odd man or a gardener and taken to the Tyneham post office at five o'clock. Later the march of civilisation caused an earlier dispatch and letters had to be in the box provided for them in the hall by three o'clock, when a kitchen messenger set out with them and left them in the village on the way to the farm to fetch the milk for tea.

The strip of grass between the road and Tizzard's was sheltered from the sea winds by a thicket of Lord Montagu's tea-plant and a bent old ash, which shaded the patient donkey while we bathed.

Fern Hollow was the home of the Charlie Millers and a very snug and hospitable home they made of it. It faced the sunrise and a view of Baltington Hill and was protected from the gales by the high, scrub-covered bank behind it. The well-stocked garden sloped down to the stream and trapped the sunshine.

The Miller family, of Scots extraction and kinsmen of the Millers (also fishermen) of Lulworth Cove, accounted for the greater part of the Worbarrow population and shared the fishing grounds. The only boat not owned by Millers belonged to Thomas Mintern, who had "Tarry" Samways as his partner.

Joseph and Charles were brothers, sons of William whose aged widow, beautiful and dignified, lived with the Josephs. The brothers were a strikingly handsome pair, dark haired and eyed, with aquiline noses and magnificent teeth. Joe wore side whiskers and Charlie grew a fine black beard. They might have stepped straight out of the pages of some buccaneering story of the Spanish main. Their rare good looks were shared by Jane, their sister, one of Queen Victoria's housemaids. Old Mrs. William Miller liked to tell us of the time when she was in service up in London and one day idly joined a crowd outside Little St. Marylebone Church, to watch a wedding party coming out. To her surprise and delight she recognized the bridegroom as my father.

Charlie's and Joseph's cousin, Henry, lived under Gold Down, up a "drong" behind the coastguard station, with his wife Louisa and their bachelor son Tom. Their younger son had married and was living in the smaller of two cottages on Baltington land across the Gwyle. The other house was occupied by the Mintern family. Jack Miller had driven the station omnibus for the Victoria Hotel at Swanage and married the Victoria's competent cook, a London maiden with the—to children—fascinating name of Alice White Rose. They named their home at Worbarrow "White Rose Cottage" and lived in it until, after Joseph's death, they moved into his house, Sea Cottage, on the edge of the shore. Alice's sister, Emily Pink Rose, became Mrs. Ellery and ran our laundry for a while. Jack and his wife moved, at the evacuation, to a house at Langton, condemned some time before and therefore conveniently unoccupied. There they endured extremes of damp and cold in great discomfort and without complaint. Jack fell a victim to bronchitis, soon after the war, but "Miggie", crippled with arthritis, lived until 1951, her gallant spirit undefeated and her Londoner's quick tongue uncurbed. She was a generous and warm-hearted neighbour and a faithful friend, whose memory is treasured by a host of summer visitors to Worbarrow as well as by the old inhabitants of Tyneham.

Henry must once have had his fair share of the family good looks and Jack inherited the Miller profile, with blue eyes and thick fair hair.

The course of the Gwyle stream widened as it neared the shore. The last stretch of the road was engineered along the unfenced edge of broken ground which dropped very steeply to the water course. This grass-and-bramble-filled ravine, with Worbarrow Tout and a small enclosure on the cliff top to the north, formed Tommy Mintern's pasturage for his active cows which scrambled up and slithered down the cliffs and stairs, clinging to ledge and scarp like so many chamois.

A tangle of Lord Montagu's tea plant hung over the road, and scattered patches of it grew along the gulley and up the opposite slope, the long and spiny sprays forming an impenetrable fence for the fishermen's gardens. The road petered out on the narrow plateau by the coastguard station with barely room to turn a car. Thence a rough footpath slippery at all times of the year ran down the steep hang to the shore. Another path, stone-bordered, pebbled and carefully weeded, led through a swing gate in a wall to the level stretch of lawn in front of the station. The children from the station came to the village school, sometimes as many as twenty or thirty at a time. In 1912, when the coastguard were withdrawn and the station closed, the loss to church and school was a heavy one. Unmarried men were rare at the Worbarrow station and caused a flutter in the Tyneham dovecotes when they joined the strength. One such disturber of the peace, Bert Wickerson, was Worbarrow's chief boatman for a number of years and a great favourite with us children. He married our head housemaid when promotion came and it was a sad day in our lives when they left for his new station.

After the coastguard went away my father had the old and inconvenient houses taken down but left the wall surrounding the enclosure.

A long block of stone made a seat on the edge of the green, at the head of the steps leading down to the fishermen's boathouse and shore. This "Council Stone" served as a look-out for mackerel and, every fine day in the season, was manned by watchers. At other times of the year the watch was kept for driftwood. My father was often to be found among the look-outs, enjoying the wise, deliberate talk beguiling the long hours of waiting. While Henry lived it was he who by sheer force of personality and by tacit consent commanded the spasmodic conversation, inspiring it with apt remarks and anecdotes, salted with wit and dry, sagacious humour. Without any education according to popular standards his mind was better furnished than that of many a Board School product whose undigested facile book-learning he held in scorn. He had learned to observe, to think and form his own opinions, and very sound and sensible they were. His rich and racy Dorset

55

dialect gave flavour to his reminiscences and he had a genius for the choice of the right word. In the Crimean War he had served as a coastal watcher, armed with a "stick with a sharp ons' end", and he had many tales to relate of his nightly patrols. The next generation were as long-headed and shrewd as Henry but "schooling" in their case had to a certain extent replaced their native sense and personal judgment.

As Henry was our gamekeeper and boatman to the House we saw far more of him than of the other fishermen and treasured many of his sayings, alas now long since forgotten.

The Miller family's intimate knowledge of the sea and of their own particular stretch of coast was not surprising in that it was an inherited lore, slowly acquired and tested, often through bitter experience. The inshore waters were their means of livelihood and gave them, if not affluence, at least sufficient comfort and contentment, breeding a tough and independent race of men who made their own important contribution to a free and self-supporting England. One cannot but count it a misfortune that these men are gone and with them all their hardly purchased knowledge of the sea and weather lore. The carefully treasured secrets of the Worbarrow fishing grounds are now destroyed.

The hauls of mackerel, though they sometimes numbered up to five or six thousand fish, were a modest summer harvest for the men, helped out by salmon peel, pout, pollock whiting, and mullet both grey and red, caught on lines. But lobster catching was the industry on which the Millers counted for their regular income. Steady supplies of lobsters and a smaller number of crabs went over the hill to the Wareham dealers in all but the winter months. The Purbeck fisheries were of great antiquity and it is known that they were very active in the sixteenth century.

In 1905 the wet fish, other than herrings, mackerel, sprats and pilchards, caught at Worbarrow amounted to nineteen hundred-weight compared with Lulworth's five hundred and Swanage's eight.

From "Balaam and Balak" onwards, that is to say, when the appointed lesson telling their story had been read in church, the shoals of mackerel might appear inside the Bay at any moment. Old people could remember how, when pa'son opened the Book and began to read the familiar tale, the men would rise up from their places and steal away to hurry down to the sea. The custom was no longer followed in my youth, but great was the excitement when the season's earliest shoal was seen in the Bay, first as a darkish smudge, like the shadow of a cloud upon the water and then, for a moment, as a popply patch where the "bait", in trying to escape the mackerel, broke the surface only to be pounced on by screaming, bickering gulls. At the very first sight of the fish the watcher left the look-out and shouting to his mates ran down to the shore. The other men ran out from cottages and boat-houses and the boats, all ready at the water's edge, were launched and away in next to no time. The stern of one boat held the carefully coiled down seine. The second boat stood by prepared to run the net out and enclose the fish as they came to shallow water in pursuit of the bait. There came a moment of intense excitement just before the encirclement was complete, and there was much threshing of oars to keep the fish from turning back towards deep water. Meanwhile the women and children had arrived upon the beach and followed the boats along the water's edge to help with hauling in the catch. Sometimes the shoal got away and this involved delay while the seine was hauled in and recoiled. But when a quantity of mackerel were secured in the net the sight was one to be remembered. The fish lay quiet until they had almost reached the shore. Then all at once the water churned and broke in a hundred places simultaneously and fish leapt high into the air, their curved wet bodies glittering with all the colours of the rainbow as they flashed into the sunlight and fell back again into the seething mass below. Women ran knee deep into the waves to help support the weight of mackerel in the straining net and slowly, inch by inch, the heavy catch was dragged out of the sea and up the shelving shore.

The moment that the shoal was seen to be enclosed a telegram had left the coastguard station and very soon the dealers' carts arrived from Wareham. The fish were counted, packed in boxes and sent off to inland markets still alive and dripping from the sea. The pick of the catch could be purchased on the beach for a penny apiece and many that were left beyond the count were given to neighbours who had lent a hand. Those plump, clean mackerel, fresh out of the sea, split, cooked with oatmeal and served up with fennel sauce, are pleasant to remember. The whitebait were left lying on the pebbles for anyone who cared to pick them up and very good they were when fried all fresh.

On moonlight nights the men went conger-fishing, an exciting sport in which my brothers joined them when at home.

The prawn and lobster pots were then all made of withies and woven in winter by the fishermen themselves.

A state of armed neutrality existed between fishermen and coastguard. The former looked upon the jetsam of the sea as lawful perquisites and counted on the driftwood cast ashore to furnish timber for a quantity of purposes connected with their trade, as well as for the upkeep of their cottage fires. The coastguards' duty, on the other hand, was to stop unauthorised salvaging, and so there was perpetual rivalry, in which the "gobbies" usually got the worst of it.

Our boathouse was a solid building, walled and tiled with Tyneham stone. It stood in a recess cut back into the cliff, with louvred windows letting in a modicum of light. It served us as a dressing-room on bathing days and housed a dinghy and my brother Ralph's canoe. The bathing raft was brought ashore and stowed away at the back before the equinoctial gales. One side of the boathouse had been taken up by a sixteen-foot boat with a centre-board until my elder brother nearly lost his life in a sailing accident. The boat was then sold and sailing off that tricky stretch of coast thenceforth forbidden.

My brother and Henry Miller, great allies and both experienced seamen, went down to Weymouth to fetch back the boat from a repairing yard. They were nearly home when a squall came on them without warning and capsized the boat. Why she turned turtle as she did has never been explained. The coast was not a mile away and my brother could have reached it but stayed with Henry as the old man could not swim. They clung to the upturned keel as best they might in a rapidly rising sea.

The Lulworth coastguard look-out saw the accident and called his lifeboat out, though the distance from the Cove was such that he knew she could not be in time. The Worbarrow Station failed to notice the disaster but a fisherman who saw it happen raised the alarm. He and the other Millers launched their boats with difficulty for by then the wind and sea had risen to a dangerous height.

The Worbarrow chief officer of coastguard was away and his second in command refused to shoulder the responsibility of taking out the lifeboat without orders. While he was telephoning to headquarters for instructions the coastguards' wives had taken the boathouse key, tackled the winch and run the heavy lifeboat down the slip into the sea. They were waist deep in the water, keeping her head into the surf when their menfolk joined them and the boat was launched, too late by then to be of any use. Henry had quickly tired and would have loosed his hold, again and again, if his companion had not rallied him and held him up. The fishermen reached them only just in time. The coastguard women again showed plenty of resource and, having seen the lifeboat launched, ran back to the station, where, when the half-drowned men were carried in, good fires, hot drinks and blankets were awaiting them. My brother, who was almost dead from exposure and exhaustion, was rubbed with whisky until circulation was restored. There is no doubt that he owed his life to the women's prompt and efficient treatment.

A well-intentioned friend from Worbarrow—but not a Worbarrow man—had meanwhile run the uphill mile to the House, where he burst into the kitchen gasping : "Master Algy's drowned!" and fainted on the floor.

None of the fishermen could swim and they refused to learn, maintaining that, if drown they must, it would be better to drown quickly.

Their attitude distressed my mother and she offered prizes to the boys who learned to swim, but these were always claimed by coastguard children.

The Millers all had iron constitutions and, with the one exception of Joseph, lived to a ripe old age. Charlie was ninety-one years old when he died, his death accelerated, if not caused, by the shock and hardship of the evacuation, which he survived for a few days only.

Jack departed in his eighties, another victim of transplanting. His brother Tom lived on until he was ninety-three. On one exceptional occasion, when Henry was laid up with some minor gastric trouble, my mother took him, amongst other invalid foods, a bunch of grapes. Next day she was aghast to find that he had swallowed every one, with skins and stones complete. The fact that they had no ill effect whatsoever on the patient speaks for the toughness of the Miller digestion.

The Henry Millers' cottage figured in an episode of the first World War, when a nervous private on the look-out for invaders saw its chimney lit-up by the moon and began to snipe it. Henry no sooner heard the shots than, by his own account, he "out of bed, on dra's, down stairs and out in garden, 'lowing that they wold Zellapins had come at last".

The Tyneham property ended, oddly enough, just short of the foreshore so that the Tout and the approach to Pondfields Cove (in local parlance, Punf'ls) belonged to Grange. Sea Cottage, occupied by the Joseph Millers and afterwards by the Jacks, stood close to the shore with nothing but a narrow, buttressed path between it and the shingle. The front door had once opened on a garden at this side, but the flower beds were swallowed by the sea, the door was walled up and in latter years the only outlet from the house was by an eastern door and a rising flight of steps. An annual peppercorn rent of a shilling was paid to the Tyneham estate for the right of access. In winter the great breakers battered and pounded the retaining wall outside the cottage, drenching the roof and seaward-facing windows. A break in the boundary wall between the house end and the fisherman's boathouse held a gateway with a gate which was seldom closed. Through this was reached the slipway serving the fishermen's boats and our own.

The Bay was never suitable for bathing by non-swimmers; its shingled shore below the tide-mark shelved abruptly, dropped over unsuspected ledges and was strewn with rocks except where fishermen and coastguards kept small areas clear for launching boats.

The water was colder than it is on shallower, sandy beaches, but competent swimmers could have plenty of fun with a boat or raft as diving board. The shelving of the shore increased towards the north side of the Bay and we were not allowed to bathe beyond the mouth of the stream on account of the under-tow.

The pebbles increased in size and were more difficult to walk on towards the ending of the shingle at Cow Corner, where the sheer wall of Flowers Barrow rose out of the sea. Sometimes we trudged along the pebbles to Cow Corner at low water and it was heavy going. We were glad to leave the shore for the face of the landslide, climbing past Harry's Thorns to reach the cliff-top half-way to the summit of Rings' Hill.

We found the rocks at the foot of the Tout a tempting field for exploration, with quantities of pools which filled at each high water.

At low tide it was possible to scramble over the rocks to Inner Point and sometimes on to Outer Point, where ledges of the Tout ran out across the Bay towards Mupe Rocks in a slanting knife-edged barrier of rock. At the inshore end of the Tout the turf which clung to its side gave way to smooth-faced slabs of limestone, thirty feet above the shore. Thick tufts and cushions of thrift and kidney vetch and "Lady's fingers" grew in the crevices of the rock and shore-larks ran among them or basked on the sun warmed surfaces.

The shingle yielded skate and dogfish eggs, starfish, and cuttle-fish "backbones", the last a delicacy relished by my mother's parrot.

In coastguard days a look-out crowned the summit of the Tout, at the top of a steep and slippery footpath guarded by a rail. The little cabin windows framed magnificent views of coast line to the east and west and a long vista of the Tyneham valley tucked between its hills. A pair of cannon flanked the signal flagstaff by the look-out and were kept smartly painted by the coastguard. They were supposed to be the last surviving relics of "Great-uncle John of Grange's" sailing -boat, the "Mary", but my husband and brother believed that they originally stood inside a sham "fort" on the Baltington cliff and were fired as a signal when the "Mary" hove in sight. A frolicsome tripper pushed one over the cliff, some years ago, and there is reason to believe that the other has shared its fate.

The small cove known as Punf'ls, beyond the neck of land con-necting Tout and mainland, held a mass of jumbled rocks and pools, an excellent hunting-ground for sea-anemones and seaweeds. The cave in the side of the Tout was easily accessible but its opposite neighbour under Gold Down could only be entered from the sea on rare occasions.

It was round the point beyond the Gold Down cave that the steam-ship "South of Ireland" ran aground on Christmas Day of 1883. Her crew were keeping Christmas to such purpose that they lost their bearings in the mist and fancied they were running into Weymouth Bay. The sea was calm and passengers and crew came safe ashore in the ship's own boats. One of the number, who had been a coastguard at the Worbarrow station, climbed up the cliff and joined his former colleagues at their Christmas dinner. According to Henry Miller his appearance from the deep caused no sensation at the table, the only comment being : "Who axed *you* to come and eat your Christmas dinner along o' we?"

The shipwreck's only casualty was a steward who, in Henry's account of the affair, jumped recklessly into a boat which held the stewardess hugging a bottle of brandy to her bosom, and broke his ankle. Twenty years later, when my brother was with the "Wind-flower", studying marine biology off the Irish coast, he told the story of the "South of Ireland's" wreck, one night at dinner. The steward waiting on the party later took my brother aside and taxed him with exaggeration, admitting that he himself was the hero of the story but indignantly denying that the bottle of brandy had any part in it.

Another wreck at Worbarrow contained a cargo of women's boots from France and flower bulbs from Holland. For some years after the ship broke up the village gardens were ablaze with tulips and Tyneham girls went elegantly shod.

A capital spring rose out of the down above the coastguard station, supplied a cattle trough in Gold Down and filled a well in the dip at the foot of the Tout. This well provided water for the station. Its overflow soaked down through rushy ground into Punf'ls Cove, losing itself in the flat, round stones above the rocks.

The narrow strip of level sward between the mainland and the Tout was used as the quoit pitch for the village matches in my youth. After the closing of the Coastguard Station quoits was seldom played at Worbarrow and a pitch was made outside the east wall of the churchyard. The distant thud of the heavy iron quoits and the cheerful clink of an occasional "ringer" are sounds inseparable from my memories of Tyneham summer evenings.

At the turn of the century Tommy Mintern was still fishing with his partner, "Tarry" Samways, but both had other means of livelihood. The Minterns had a family of rosy, smiling daughters and then, at last, one son, who did not live to comfort their old age. In his seventeenth year the boy was drowned while fishing with a townsman relative of "Miggie" Miller. Poor Willie "came home", after many weary weeks of waiting on his parents' part, and was buried with their hopes in Tyneham churchyard. Another tragedy was enacted in the field above the Mintern's house, when a schoolboy grandson of the only "tenants" Tyneham House has ever had was thrown from his horse while riding there. He fell with his head against the only stone in the field and died immediately.

From White Rose Cottage and the Minterns' house a footpath crossed the little close beside the gardens, dropped to the stream and passing by the garden of Fern Hollow joined the road near Tizzards'.

We often visited Fern Hollow and its kindly mistress. The little house, well hidden by the thickets in the hollow, was in itself attractive to a child, suggesting an enchanted dwelling in a secret forest. Dense tangles of the spiny tea-plant and of crimson fuchsias shut it in and bordered the steep stairways of uneven stone which made the three approaches, one from the sea road, one from a wicket to the west, the third from across the stream.

Charles Miller's wife, a White of Kingston, had been the Tyneham school-ma'am in her maiden days and was devoted to young things but had no children of her own. We loved her bright and lively face, warm laugh and husky voice which always welcomed us. I never saw her otherwise than neat and trim, appearing at her doorway in a spotless apron. Her little house was just as clean and tidy as her person. We never tired of looking at its many photographs and treasures which Mrs. Charlie seemed to enjoy displaying. One ornament of the parlour which we dearly loved was a small stuffed tabby kitten attached to a photograph frame.

Charlie and Harriet were a devoted pair. I cherish a charming portrait of them, taken in the garden on their golden wedding day. Charlie is gallantly offering the still comely Harriet a rose, and she looks pleased and bashful. She sang in the choir for 40 years at least, walking to church twice every Sunday. Charlie was seriously ill when the evacuation fell in bitter December weather. Because of an influenza epidemic raging at the time, more than half the ambulances promised for the transport of the sick and aged failed to arrive. The Charlies were among the unfortunates compelled to wait for twenty-four hours in comfortless homes with all their household goods packed up and ready to go. The old man died, a few days later, begging my brother to take him back to Worbarrow. Permission was given for his burial at Tyneham. Harriet lingered on for several years, but all her zest for living had departed with her home and Charlie. When she, too, died, it was impossible to bury her remains with his and so they rest in Wareham churchyard.

Henry was spared the ordeal of uprooting, for he died in 1926. He outlived his Louisa for a number of years and was devotedly cared for by his granddaughter, a daughter's child, until his death. She afterwards kept house for her Uncle Tom, at Worbarrow and in the cottage found for them at Kimmeridge.

The Gwyle stream furnished eels—diminutive creatures—for the baiting of lines (a sliver of eel was irresistible to mackerel) and the fishermen would search the "lake" bed for them, turning up stones and catching the elvers with their hands. Henry made use of his hat, a battered affair without colour or shape, as a creel, replacing it on his bald head between catches with a time-honoured joke about "they girt, wold eëls as had ate all his hair off".

Although we loved our mornings by the sea, the Worbarrow picnics which my mother organised for visitors and neighbours were less popular with her children. By late afternoon the westering sun was low enough to take the colour from the Bay and made a dazzle of the sea. The Sunday clothes we wore in honour of our guests were not conducive to enjoyment among rocks and pools—black, buttoned boots instead of sandshoes*, ribbed wool stockings, well starched frocks and flopping hats which strained at their elastic moorings in the wind. The little waggon, loaded with a table to be set up in the boathouse, with crockery and urn and baskets full of food, set out ahead of us, escorted by a footman, to prepare the spread. The boiling water for the urn was supplied by Mrs. Jack.

My mother had a passion for the sea and was a maddeningly perfect sailor, a quality unshared by her less nautically minded daughters. On long sea transits she was in her element and never missed a meal how-

---

* Old English for plimsolls.

ever wild the weather, leaving her suffering offspring languishing below. I am sure she thought our misery imaginary. On one occasion, voyaging in a gale from Malta to Marseilles in a decrepit *Transatlantique* liner, my parent, a French admiral and a British one, the late Lord Wester Wemyss, became the sole survivors to appear at the dinner table and when Sir Rosslyn, as he then was, finally succumbed, my mother was left to uphold the honour of our British seamanship alone.

There was nothing she more enjoyed than an outing in the dinghy or Henry's boat, and any excuse would serve for a trip by sea. Sometimes, in party bibs and tuckers, we rowed to Arishmel and walked from there to Lulworth, East or West, to visit friends. Sometimes our guests, their ill-assumed enthusiasm thinly veiling their reluctance, were taken to admire the "fossil forest" in the cliff above Mupe Bay and on to Lulworth Cove for tea at the Cove Hotel. Slowly returning, always (it seemed to us) in the teeth of wind and tide, with 'flop' or ground swell hideously apparent, our thoughts revolved around the pleasant fare we had so recently enjoyed. We sat in paralysed silence while my mother carried on an animated conversation with the oarsman. At intervals in the ghastly three-mile transit Henry would rest upon his oars to point out some inaccessible fox earth in the cliff or some repellent sea fowl circling giddily overhead. Then the afflicting rhythm of the oars would begin again, the sickening squeak and thump accentuated by the compound odours from the bilge awash beneath the floorboards. Henry would mock our sufferings, saying that "thic wold boat have belonged to I for fifty years and he an't learned eet to keep hisself quiet when I do tell un to".

On certain days of the week a paddle-boat from Weymouth visited Lulworth Cove, picking up passengers for Weymouth and returning them a few hours later. My parents loved this expedition, which involved a walk to Worbarrow, followed by three miles' rowing over the Bay to Lulworth. If winds and tides were against them they would disembark at Arishmel and walk over Swine's Back to the east shore of the Cove, whence they would signal to a Lulworth boat to come and fetch them. After some hours in Weymouth they returned as they had gone.

During the equinoctial gales, whenever it was possible to stand against the wind, we fought our way to Worbarrow to watch the monster seas come rolling in. I still feel the exhilaration of plunging out into the storm and trying my strength against the force of the tempest. We leaned our whole weight on the pressure of the gusts, which snatched our breath away and often brought us to a standstill or whipped us off our feet and sent us tumbling backwards. Shouted remarks were lost in the roaring of the gale as it cuffed our ears and buffetted our faces, filling our gasping mouths with the salt taste of the sea. When we tired of the struggle at last and turned our backs to the wind, what fun it was to run before it, light and effortless as autumn leaves, reaching the shelter of the House with skins aglow and muscles tingling from the exercise.

It was a splendid spectacle when the towering seas assaulted Mupe, smothering the stacks of rock and sending great sheets of spray to the top of the cliff. The noise of the breakers pounding on the Worbarrow shore and the roar of the shingle sucked down by the under tow was deafening. Fritters and sponges of yellowish foam were driven far along the valley and lodged against the hedges, banks and walls. My sister remembers a sou'wester which left quantities of dabs caught up in the bushes of the Hole Field Leg.

In summer, after bathing, it was difficult to keep from nodding over our lessons in the afternoon, but even in holiday time my mother discouraged any form of idleness. How often has she come upon me curled up in a chair with a fascinating book and briskly asked : "Well now, my dear, can't you find something better to do?" With her, jobs that needed to be done abounded whether in house or garden, or one might be sent off on Samaritan errands to far distant cottages. She liked us to take part in social doings with the neighbours and, looking back, I fear that our reluctance to play up to her arrangements for our pleasure must often have caused her disappointment. Her Yorkshire upbringing had given her a dislike for anything in the way of lounging and I cannot remember ever having seen her, even in extreme old age, with her feet up on a sofa. She did give in at last to doctors and relations to the extent of taking a brief rest in her armchair after luncheon, but that remained her utmost concession to inaction.

As long as her sight allowed she was a skilful needle-woman and she knitted for Queen Mary's Needlework Guild up to within a few months of her death. Her correspondence occupied a large share of her time. She wrote to her younger sister every day until the latter's death and to her absent children nearly as often. Meticulous about the answering of letters, she seldom kept a correspondent waiting more than a post for her reply. Very often in my long life I have wished that other correspondents, private and official, were half as businesslike and conscientious. Until she grew too blind she never failed to write me a daily letter in her beautiful clear and characteristic hand.

She used to say that when she first lived in the south she found the slow, deliberate movements of the southern people hard to bear with. Later she came to realise how far the climate influenced the tempo of men's daily life, but I have often wondered how she would react to what in post-war days is known as "working".

CHAPTER VII

Woods, Cliffs and Fields

THE summer evenings of my childhood hold for me the happiest of all my Tyneham memories. Those hours between our tea and bedtime, free from lessons and restraint, were times of perfect bliss and peace. Because, I suppose, the sunny days brought most enjoyment, they are the ones most clearly printed on my memory, the wet or foggy evenings tend to be forgotten. To cast my mind back to the summers of my youth is to see golden sunlight on the hills and woods and lengthening bars of shadow lying across the avenue alternately with glowing shafts of light.

The avenue made a favourite starting-point for a haphazard ramble, sometimes in quest of rabbits for the pot or for the ferrets' dinner, but preferably without a gun and with a quiet dog for company. "Amos" was my companion for a number of years, a peaceable Scots' terrier who could be relied upon to follow close at heel and "freeze" when I stood still. He could be conversational at other times and I have never known another dog who "talked" as he did, voicing his emotions in low gurglings and mutterings of infinite variety. His loud and hearty yawn, embracing a whole scale of notes, was his most personal accomplishment, a startling affair to those whom it took unawares.

His grave is one of a group in a corner of the orchard bordering on the Avenue which is the resting-place of many cherished pets—dogs, ferrets, cats and "Blitz", our trotting donkey. A block of stone engraved "Goliath" marks the grave of a beloved ferret, the wallydraggle of a litter, small, plucky and down-trodden by his family and on that account made much of by his owners. Our care of him was well rewarded when he grew into a handsome polecat ferret with an unusual silvery undercoat. He learned to answer to his name and went for walks with us on a collar and lead, to the amusement of our neighbours. His mother outlived her twenty-three sons and daughters and "Jezebel", her sister, produced over forty lively children which we sold at the current price of half-a-crown apiece

My father's Labrador retrievers and a spaniel of my mother's were among the many dogs interred in the orchard cemetery. I think we were most fortunate, as children, in our parents' love of animals. From our earliest days we were surrounded by all kinds of animal friends and taught to love and understand them. I cannot remember being without some pet to feed and care for. The long list of our favourites included rabbits, dormice, bantams, bullfinches, canaries, Java sparrows, piglets, donkeys, ponies, cats, dogs, ferrets, lambs, Japanese mice, young gulls and ravens found with injured wings, ducks, tortoises (both land and water), tree frogs, tadpoles, sticklebacks and goldfish. My mother had her parrots and tame pigeons and every year she reared young partridges and pheasants from the nests of eggs discovered in the hay grass by the mowers The feeding of these youngsters meant a ceaseless hunt for ants' "eggs" and the summer task most often laid upon us was the quest, with trowel, spade and bucket, for "emmut butts" containing "eggs".

We all inherited my mother's love for many and unusual pets but my brother Ralph came in for by far the largest share. When travelling round the world in 1900 he bought a tethered sparrow-hawk from a market in Peking and carried it home by way of North America to give to the London Zoo, which later he enriched with a young giraffe from his own Sudanese collection His private Zoo contained, at different periods, two kinds of monkey, three varieties of gazelle, a crocodile, a wart-hog, kudu, elephant, porcupines, hyenas, cranes, ostriches and electric fish His flock of geese inhabited the Avenue at Tyneham while he lived there and his children added guinea pigs to the roll of family pets.

The Great Wood kept the orchard, sandwiched as it was in between the Hole Field and the Avenue, safe from easterly winds. The trees had grown so tall that they overshadowed it and the apple trees were old and unproductive. In earlier days they must have yielded a considerable crop, as is witnessed in a pleasant story told me by my cousin and brother-in-law, John Wentworth Garneys Bond of Grange. When a young man, perhaps in the eighteen-eighties or the early 'nineties, he walked from Grange with a friend to call upon his Tyneham kinsmen At the House they were directed to the orchard, where they found great-uncles John and Tom watching the picking and sorting of the apples The friend was fascinated by the picture of the two old brothers, silver-haired, top-hatted, in black suits, black shoes and snowy socks, surrounded by the baskets of bright fruit all glowing in the autumn sunlight, and he never forgot it He felt he had been given the rare privilege of looking back into a world before his time and sometimes wondered whether he had really had the glimpse of the two old men in the peaceful scene or whether the picture was a dream of the brothers Cheeryble in an ideal setting.

My father planted golden willows in the orchard and my brother added to them while he lived at Tyneham.

A gate by the orchard opened into the main ride of the wood, a wide grassed carriage-way made for my great-aunts Jane and Mary, so that they might be driven in the landau to the Ocean Seat. The first two hundred yards or so of ride was planted on either side with double poetaz narcissus, associated in my mind with Trinity Sunday and its altar decorations as firmly as the scarlet azalea is with Whitsuntide. The strong scent of the close white flower heads still evokes a compound picture of sunlit chancel and of Cherubim and Seraphim "casting down their golden crowns around the glassy sea".

66

Wood sedges grew with the narcissus, and hard fern dipped into the little water course beside the road.

About half way up the slope, between the avenue and the ride, was a small enclosure planted with Douglas spruce and larch, intended by my father as a windscreen for young deciduous trees put in to fill a gap in the Avenue made by a disastrous gale. The whole of this plantation was destroyed by the "army of occupation".

Along the borders of the Avenue and scattered through the wood the stinking iris (most maligned of wild flowers) flourished in its pride of glossy, orange berries, a gay addition to the Christmas evergreens in the years when holly failed us.

Not far from this first stretch of ride I found the remnants of the only dormouse nest I ever saw at Tyneham. Dormice, like frogs and nightingales, were almost non-existent in the valley.

A pair of buzzards nested every year in the silver firs behind the orchard, at a time when buzzards were far less common than they are to-day. The Gadcliff foxes had a thoroughfare which crossed the carriage drive. We saw them using it from time to time and often scented them. From the top of the Avenue the ride turned sharply to the south to slant up through the wood. Here at the angle was a bench which made a pleasant resting-place. Horse chestnuts, grown from seed by my younger sister and myself, grew close at hand, with a copper beech of my father's planting. But all this part of the wood was a camp site during the war and the beech was among the many trees destroyed.

On either side of the ride the earliest primroses appeared, always before the Christmas holidays and sometimes in October and November, a welcome sight against their background of bright moss and vivid ivy leaves, orange, maroon and scarlet like some exquisite enamel. This corner of the wood abounded in anemones, wood spurge and blue-bells, barren strawberries, violets, moschatel and orchis—early purple, pyramid and butterfly—in their several seasons. The grey-green sprays of honeysuckle garlanded the pathways at the dead end of the year though, truth to tell, there never was a period of deadness in the woods at Tyneham. Before the last of the lingering autumn leaves had fluttered to the ground "lamb's tails" were showing on the hazel twigs and rose-red female flowers appeared soon after. In very early spring dogs' mercury pushed up between the "mocks", clothing the soil with fresh and tender green and eaten by the dogs with manifest enjoyment.

Some distance up the rise another bench invited climbers to enjoy the view across the tree tops to the hill against the northern sky. The hazels covering the slope above the seat concealed some ruined brick-work in a hollow of the ground, the remnants of a cache where spirits, run ashore in Brandy Bay below the Ocean Seat, were temporarily hidden. One summer night my father's grandfather was sitting in the library alone, the servants having locked the outside doors and gone to bed, when he heard a whisper at the open window, advising him to leave the key in the cellar door that night. He kept his eyes on his book, affecting to hear nothing, and, it is scarcely necessary to say, refused the tempting sop.

When I was young the only patch of ramsons or wild garlic in the Great Wood grew where the Wood merged with the West Plantation. About the 'thirties it began to spread and in a very short time had almost overrun the Wood. The fresh green lance-shaped leaves and snowy heads of flowers looked, at a little distance, like wild lilies-of-the-valley. Only at closer quarters did the plant's rank smell destroy its charm, clinging persistently to shoes and garments which had brushed against it. The heavy odour of the leaves when crushed would taint the air and drift to a considerable distance. The ramsons flourished in the Gwyle and, at certain seasons, flavoured hens' eggs at the farm.

Where Wood and West Plantation joined, the Hole Field Leg, a narrow belt of trees and copse, projected to the north, dividing the Hole Field and Eweleaze. Stunted maples, sycamores and oaks grew in the Leg, blown slantwise by the prevailing wind. Their twisted branches formed a shelter for the path through day lilies and montbretias whose dense reedy foliage made a favourite nesting place for pheasants.

To my young mind the little Hole Field embraced by trees was the spot that I pictured as the Psalmist's *"campus silvae"*. No meddling hand had tried to tame or tidy it, and its rough, lovely wildness was in charming contrast with the formal garden at its foot. The lower portion, just outside the Avenue and lawn, was shaded by a grove of elms and underneath the ancient trees the grass was gay in spring with many kinds of sweet-scented narcissus, amongst them the old-fashioned "butter-and-eggs", since lost to the world through bulb growers' "improvements". As the field steepened to the south the pasture ended in a hang of rough grass sheltering early cowslips, to begin again on a level plateau under the Wood. Clusters of hawthorns broke the line of the slope, foaming with blossom in May and crimson-berried in the autumn. Those farthest from the House stood grouped about a spring and pool in the hollow whence the field derived its name. My father tapped the spring to supply the House and built a reservoir to hold eight thousand gallons under the thicket.

The best sloes for the annual vintage of sloe gin came from the tangled blackthorn hedge dividing field and wood. A wicket breached the hedge and led into the Lower Hole Field Ride, to me the pleasantest in all the wood. The thick moss underfoot made silent progress easy and so ensured a sight of the profusion of wild life inhabiting the undergrowth. Here titmice came in numbers to be fed on scraps and crumbs, and here was the stone trough sunk into the soft ground by my brother, to catch the water from a tiny spring. The drinking-place was visited by birds and animals of many kinds, including deer whose sharp-toed slots were left imprinted in the clay.

The Great Wood had been lovingly laid out before the days when the customary way of planting is "in numbered blocks, like melancholy

squads awaiting execution". Its limited acreage held infinite variety,
from the high wood of the West Plantation to the oaks of the lower
stands and the tempest toughened ashes, elms and sycamores along the
southern wall, streamlined by many gales until they flowed towards
the east like weeds in the current of a river.

Parts of the soil were carpeted with ivy, others with sedges, and
where the older blocks of copse-wood stood the ground was bare of
vegetation.

The aspect of each section changed from year to year as the copse-
wood cuts were made in due rotation, so that each area in succession
was laid open to the sun and air, slowly grew over and in time became
thick covert once again. Trees which had been surrounded and concealed by copsewood suddenly emerged, like welcome friends returning
after a long absence. Tall groves of ash were left to mature until the
poles were thick and strong enough for fencing. The hazel "mocks"
were shorn more often for their pea and bean sticks and for firewood.
The estate was self-supporting in so far as pea and bean sticks for the
House and village gardens were concerned. All timber for the bars
and gate-posts, hurdle stakes and wreath for fencing came out of the
coverts, and each cottage in the village had its woodshed filled with
faggots "against the winter".

The quality that I associate before all others with the Great Wood
on those golden summer evenings is its utter stillness. We had our
share and more of windy weather and no day in the summer was without a breeze at some time or another but, often enough, the light air
dropped as the afternoon wore on and not a leaf stirred in the valley.
The quiet was such as it is rare to come across in these machine-
tormented days. No noise from road or railway troubled that peace,
no drone of aircraft and no sound of human industry save that of
quiet country occupations, heard as an echo faint and mellowed by
distance.

In harvest time, when men were out late in the fields, their voices
blended with the quietude and did not break it as the racket of machin-
ery can shatter it to-day. In that encompassing silence the delicate
woodland sounds came clear to the ear, each one distinct, the tiny
splash and trickle of some travelling thread of water hidden in the
mosses, the far-off tapping of a woodpecker, the sudden hum of a
passing insect or the low call-note of a bird. A rustle in the fallen
leaves betrayed the stealthy movements of a shrew about his personal
affairs, or an unseen squirrel might drop an empty nutshell pattering
through the branches. Again, the myriad voices of the wood like the
sounds of life outside were in harmony with the all-embracing silence,
serving to emphasize its pure intensity. The mind, receptive and
attuned, absorbed the quietness and at last was saturated with its peace.
This woodland quiet was no negative thing—a simple absence of all
bustle and noise—but a positive presence leaving an indelible impression. It seems to me that the grave and steady temper of mind, the deep

tranquillity which characterised the valley dwellers in so marked a manner, came through an uninterrupted contact with the woods and fields and hills.

To me, at least, the Wood was one of those "ultimate places" where, as Belloc says, "things common become shadows and fail, and the divine part in us which adores and desires, breathes its own air and is at last alive".

The first of the Tyneham woodmen that I remember was a Balson, whose son was his assistant for a time. Old Balson was a little, wiry man as gnarled and woody-looking as a tree root. His clothes, well weathered by long use, were the traditional corded leggings and thick leather coat topped by a round and ear-flapped headdress of brown fur. His eyes looked east and west, unsynchronised, and with his straggling whiskers and sparse locks he might have been some sylvan wildling out of mythical times, in perfect harmony with his environment. He never learned to read and write, or had forgotten what he learned, but, if required to make some piece of household joinery, a rabbit hutch or kennel, he listened carefully to the directions, made mental notes and, using his belt for making measurements, produced a neat and accurate piece of handiwork. His home was in the heath at Povington and he walked to his work, taking as near as possible a bee line over the hill. The track worn by his daily journeys in the course of the years outlasted him for many more, and the place in the hedge where he climbed from the North Hill into Madmore continued, long after his death, to be known as Balson's Gap.

Balson's successor, William Taylor, was a competent woodman with an excellent working knowledge of his craft. Sparing of speech—like most true men of the woods?—he seemed to enjoy the loneliness of his calling but owned that, in earlier days, when copsing deep in Yellowham Wood, he found the solitude and silence there oppressive. Working all day in the remoter, twilit parts of that vast acreage of trees he often heard no sound for hours, beyond the daytime hooting of the owls.

On certain evenings, when "the gentleness of heaven was on the sea", the pull of the cliffs proved even stronger than the enchantments of the woods. A short cut from the House to the Ocean Seat traversed the Rookery Wood and West Plantation, a zigzag route whose gradients did not trouble our accustomed legs though apt to cause a stranger to show symptoms of distress. The first lap took us through the Rookery Wood, a cool and airy place of lofty trees and knee-deep ivy.

The rooks had a preference for the top of the wood, remaining faithful to the same high chestnuts, elms and ashes, but now and again a nest or two would appear in a tree some distance down the Plot and even so far from the parent colony as the Gwyle above the Farm. The old nests were repaired and reinhabited each spring, giving no colour to the common theory that the level of the nests foretells the weather for the year.

The wood fell away downhill to the Worbarrow road in miniature cascades of glistening harts' tongue ferns. It held a dipping-well of cold spring water, set in a deep recess by the roadside, entered by a wicket gate and roofed with stone.

Here, in perpetual green shade, the air was cool and sweet with the scent of ferns and water-sprinkled mosses.

From the top of the wood the way to the Ocean Seat struck up across the Eweleaze, through the West Plantation and out again into the upper portion of the Eweleaze, thence through a bridle gate to Twelve Acres. Stone steps in the wall beside the gate remained to mark the church path from South Egliston used before the gate was in existence.

The Ocean Seat was sheltered by high mortared walls of undressed stone on every side except the south where they gave way to a low stone parapet. Here one might sit and watch the shipping passing up and down the Channel or find a store of entertainment in the ways of the cliff-haunting birds. An occupant of the seat was so well hidden by its walls that ravens, peregrines and gulls would often fly within a few feet of the watcher before they sighted him and swerved away.

Between the peregrine and ravens there was a constant feud, or was it sport? Their aerial skirmishings and acrobatics were a fascinating sight, each splendid bird manoeuvring and jockeying for a place above his rival, to the sound of grumbling bass notes from the ravens and knife-edged screams from the agile, light-winged falcons.

The boundaries of Tyneham and South Tyneham met by the Ocean Seat and a stile in the dividing wall let through the coastguard path along the cliffs. When all the stations on the coast were manned, as they were when I was young, each station contacted its next-door neighbours twice every twenty-four hours. The path they used was often dangerously near the edge of the cliff and it was marked for safety by a line of heavy stones kept freshly whitewashed as a guide in foggy weather and to reflect the light of lanterns carried by the men on night patrol. The endless chain of whitened stones forsook the cliff top at the Ocean Seat and followed a grassy ledge upon the shoulder of Tyneham Gap. These stones have long since disappeared, pushed over the cliff by irresponsible holiday makers.

The little triangle of rowaty grass which hung on the brow of the precipice west of the boundary was known as Sedge Plot. At this point Gadcliff's towering bastion ended suddenly and the limestone rock of the cliff gave place to Kimmeridge clay. The contour of the cliff abruptly sank from a height of some 500 feet to the low and even line of shale extending eastwards beyond Brandy Bay. The shore could be reached from Tyneham Cap by a rough and breakneck path, passing a ledge with a drinking place for cattle grazing on South Tyneham. Repeated rock falls from the overhanging cliff had covered an extensive area of the undercliff and made the journey to the Smugglers' Cave an arduous one. The cave was so well hidden that even those who knew it and the guiding landmarks well could easily miss it. The Waggon Rock, an oblong, flat-topped block, was one of the more conspicuous of these clues ; a smaller stone, completely covered with ivy, was another.

The entrance to the cache was through a narrow passage tunnelled under a rock, with a drop of some feet from the end of it to the floor of the hollow chamber. The first to crawl in through the hole required some courage in view of the stories of foxes at bay and of other inhabitants even less pleasing discovered by earlier explorers. When the leader was in and his candle well alight the crawl through the entrance was robbed of half its thrill for those who came after. Four or five people could squeeze themselves into the cave with middling discomfort, but only the smallest could stand at full height. It was hardly the place for a subject of claustrophobia. The agelong minutes while a stout companion struggled through the passage, blocking the only source of air, were none too pleasant to a keen imagination. There was one dreadful day when a friend, with a breadth to match his six foot three of height, stuck firmly in the tunnel and, for what seemed like an eternity of horror, appeared unlikely ever to move again, in spite of the frenzied efforts of the imprisoned to push him out, my mother meanwhile tugging from outside to save her loved ones.

What looked like scrub and furze from the top of Gadcliff was sizeable wood at the foot of the scarp, a favourite haunt of foxes. On summer evenings an excellent view of the cubs at play by their earth could be had from the edge of the cliff. The South Dorset Hunt avoided the valley, having lost several hounds on the cliffs. The Hunt and landlords had an understanding that the race of foxes harbouring in Gadcliff must, by whatever means, be kept within bounds. So once or twice in the year the gamekeepers from Grange, with Henry Miller, George the postman and a farmer or two, assembled with a motley pack of tough, enthusiastic dogs and assaulted rocks and thickets with the maximum of peril to all concerned. The edge of the cliff made an excellent grand stand well out of gunshot range.

From below, the ledge where the ravens nested under a vertical bluff, could easily be seen. The crag overhung the nest so far as to make it safe from interference from above, and it was almost as inaccessible from the shore, so making easier the task, inherited through many generations, of giving sanctuary to the noble birds. The cliff birds set up such a clamour when molested that, as a rule, intruders could be interrupted before serious harm was done, though sometimes would-be sportsmen came in from the sea and slaughtered gulls and guillemots with rifles, maiming far many more than they destroyed outright.

Late August and September drew us to the South Hill pastures, where the mushroom crop was heaviest. There was a time when mushrooms were prolific in the Egliston Meads but when the meads were given a coat of basic slag, the dressing then becoming all the fashion, mushrooms disappeared and never came again.

To reach the hill we crossed the nearer Eweleaze, passing the iron target set against the hillside for the coastguards' rifle and revolver practice and used by us for practice with a rook rifle. The bull's eye was a square of iron, lightly hung, and made a satisfying clang when hit, proclaiming a successful shot to all the corners of the parish.

Great puffballs grew occasionally in the Eweleaze and were good to eat when sliced and fried in butter *aux fines herbes*.

I call to mind still autumn days when the whole surface of the field was covered by a rippling sea of gossamer, broken by milk-white waves of cobweb-covered tufts of grass. The shimmering counterpane had much in common with the lather of the low sea fogs, filling the valley while the hills stayed clear. But whereas the fog clouds, seen from up above, appeared as firm and spoonable as clotted cream, the veil of gossamer had all the lightness and translucency of fine, spun glass, each of the myriad delicate threads refracting the sun's rays, flashing and sparkling with the motion of the imperceptible airs.

The best of the mushroom fields was New Ground, entered by the uphill waggon track from Tyneham Farm. How many early autumn evenings I remember in those grass lands high above our miniature world, happily occupied in filling baskets until it grew too dark to tell the mushrooms from the scattered stones, and mushrooms, grass and shoes were soaked with dew.

The sound of voices, softened by distance from the village, rose through the motionless air, and the wheels of a travelling tradesman's cart, a mile away along the road, could be distinctly heard.

The South Hill fields led one into another, on the landward side by gates and bars, on the cliff top by rough stiles across the coast-guards' path. The cliff had fallen away in places, and at least one stile had drawn uncomfortably near the edge. A wide unculti-vated strip between the tillage and the cliff was annually inhabited by swarms of burnet moths, sluggishly clinging to the bents. When brushed off by a passing foot they fluttered clumsily a yard or so and settled again.

The central backbone of the valley held its own attractions. The hedge between Old Cowleaze Knap and Starveall, the North Egliston plough ground, grew in a smother of sweet honeysuckle and the bank was thick with foxgloves. Rails in the north-east corner of the Knap provided a short cut for walkers over Buffknolls into the Wareham road.

The first of the Egliston Meads marched with the Old Cowleaze and was the watershed, the source of the two streamlets which with the Long Coppice Water formed the property's irrigation system. East-ward the little Corfe river started on its devious course through field and farm to reach the heath at last and spill into Poole Harbour. The Tyneham water turned its back upon its fellow to begin its mile and a quarter journey to the sea, so small at first that its voice, like the tinkling of a tiny musical-box, was scarcely audible except to an attentive ear delighting in the ever-recurring theme of "glip, glup, glippety glip, glop, goggle, tonk!" so meek that a handful of dead leaves deflected it or formed a teacup pool where inch-deep waterfalls spilled over with the gentlest of splashes.

But after storms the surface water from the Wood transformed the trickle to a noisy torrent, tumbling and foaming down the Avenue to the haha ditch and diving under the lawn and Stable Plot to emerge beside the Worbarrow road and join its sister stream at Toadstile for the last rush to the sea. The Long Coppice tributary fed the sheep wash and the village pond on its way to the meeting place.

When I first knew the Tyneham River it was unfenced along the sea road in the Rookery Wood. Retaining walls upheld the bank in several places and a false step in the dark would have meant a four or five foot drop to the stones in the bed of the stream. My father fenced a hundred yards of the road with a line of posts and a single rail, a hollow pipe which made an intriguing whispering gallery for the young of succeeding generations.

The drinking places in the Egliston Meads were the young Corfe River's first appearance in the outer world. They both began their lives as muddy splashes overgrown with rushes, where stock could drink in rainy seasons only. After my father had them deepened, walled and paved with stone they held a good supply of water and did not fail the cattle save in exceptional droughts. The lower pond attracted moorhens and they bred close by in several seasons.

A curious extension of the second Mead projected for a hundred yards or so into North Egliston Cowleaze. This little strip, called Chapel Close, was said to be the site of an ancient chapel and still showed traces of foundations, though these may well have been remains of cottages and gardens of a later date.

A stile in the boundary fence near the second pond led into a drong and track connecting Egliston Farm with its pastures on the south side of the hill, for each of the valley farms included part of the North Hill and a strip of grass land running down towards the sea.

A string of gateways, bars and stiles marked out the way across the farms to Steeple Church and rectory, a wettish walk in winter but at other times a pleasant two-mile stretch of grass fields gay with cowslips, buttercups or ox-eye daisies. For part of the way the path lay across the cowleazes at Lutton, my family's first home in Purbeck. A younger scion of the Bonds at Erth, near Saltash, moved eastward into Somerset and settled at Hatch Beauchamp. Thence one of his descendants came to Purbeck and married, in 1431, the heiress of the Luttons.

Passing by Steeple Church the footpath cut across the remaining farms, Blackmanston, Bradle, Orchard (West and East) and Bucknowle to come out on the Halves at Corfe, a five mile walk remote from traffic.

74

The footpath was a courtesy one, no right of way, and it is perhaps unnecessary to remark that the courtesy was returned and the path unused while pastures were laid up for hay.

The north side of the Tyneham property possessed a set of wild flowers and a charm of its own, distinct from the attractions of the Great Wood and South Hill. Long Coppice and Rook Grove Field were rich with bright marsh marigolds, the "May blobs" of the children, and the Sheep-wash at the lower end of Long Coppice was hedged about with greater willow-herb. The muddy margin of the pool held tracks of many animals and birds which came to drink there.

The footpath from the bottom of Wayground on the Wareham road kept close to Long Coppice, passed the sheep-wash into Three Acres and over a culvert into Rook Grove Field. Skirting the field it passed another barway, entered the North Cowleaze and so arrived at Church and village.

Three Acres, which in my early days I took to be the original Ideal Home of Mr. Gladstone's cow, was one of the fields for which I had a special fondness. The little plot lay snug and lew between its three stout hedges and the deep tree-shaded gulley of the Long Coppice stream. It had a friendly welcoming look at all times of the year and most of all when it was under hay. The flowers of the hayfield here grew extra strong and sweet, buttercup, ox-eye daisy, sorrel, cathartic flax, clover, hop clover, medick, bird's foot trefoil, scabious, salad burnet, pasture lousewort, yellow rattle, bartsia, eyebright, speedwell, milfoil, hawkbit, mouse-ear hawkweed, spurry, quaking grass, rest-harrow and a host of others. One of the willows by the stream hung over the bridge between the little close and Rook Grove Field, combing the passing waggon-loads of hay.

A tiny water course, from Long Mead under the hills, bisected Rook-Grove Field, dived through a "bunny" under the village-going path and helped to make a miniature pool where it joined the Long Coppice water. The excellent grazing ground of Rook Grove Field was gay with cowslips, Lady's smocks and the spires of early purple, spotted and pyramidal orchis in the spring.

How or when Rook Grove got its name I do not know. The covert never held a rookery in my time or my father's. The roedeer loved its southern aspect and so did the woodcock, while its sunny glades showed primroses in flower the whole year round.

A spring and reservoir above the Grove supplied the village with a steady flow of pure and sparkling water, never known to fail except on one occasion, when officers were living in the rectory in 1943 and tapped the pipe, leaving the village without water. A number of courteous protests from my brother remained unanswered until, after several weeks had passed, a seventh letter (stronger and rougher like the seventh wave) produced the visit of an envoy from H.Q. at Winchester, a kindly, puzzled man who, having little by little grasped the facts and recognized the urgency of the case, proposed that his Department should "pay the water-rate". Hard as this tale may be to swallow it has its counterpart in which the principle actors were four officers of the R.A.F. who came to inspect the House before the Air Force took it over. My brother's wife, who showed them round, laid stress on the scarcity of water, remarking that, in the summer months, available supplies would barely meet the needs of a small family, whereas the R.A.F. proposed that the House should shelter sixty W.A A F's. The officers assured her that she need not worry, as many more lavatories and bathrooms would certainly be provided.

Incredible though this may seem it is not very far removed from the attitude of some who hold it against country landlords that their tenants are still dependent for their water on a well, in places where available resources are inadequate for the provision of running water for each house. This is a boon which all must hope will come, and come eventually it doubtless will, at vast expense to public funds. To ask the landlord to effect the improvement without help is, in a case like that of Tyneham, to demand impossibilities.

Great-uncle John who, when Vicar of Weston, brought spring water from the hills below Bath race-course to supply his parish, was also responsible for the Madmore reservoir at Tyneham and piped the water to the village fountain.

The field adjoining Long Mead to the west was called Church Furlong and its narrow strip on the further side of the Lulworth road was know as Flagon Grass. Perhaps because when the hayfield acreage was reckoned up for mowers' pay, this small irregular plot was settled for in liquid kind?

Church Furlong still showed traces of the village cultivation of an early, probably Saxon, date.

The path between House and village was well worn and, on the slope of the Cowleaze, frequently washed out, so that lanterns were an indispensable accessory for church goers after dark. The whole way to the village from the House was open to the south-west wind and often difficult to traverse. Sometimes the House men on their way to and from their work were forced to follow a circuitous course, keeping to leeward of the hedges to avoid being blown down by the gusts. We had special baskets made for carrying flowers and greenery to church, of a length and depth sufficient to protect long stems and branches. Even so the wind would sometimes snatch away the contents. Umbrellas were of little use and nothing but oilskins and sou'westers, gaiters and goloshes, could keep out the weather. On wet and windy Sundays much disrobing and rerobing occupied the back pews of the transepts, where an array of dripping garments were spread out to dry during service time. Hats oftentimes vanished in the darkness on the way to Evensong and were never seen again. Often the hurricane lamps we carried would be 'douted' by the gale and then we had to find our way by trial and error, colliding with furze bushes and fences. Cows had a tiresome habit too, of sleeping on the path. My elder sister once fell over an obstruction which sprang bellowing and snorting to its feet, more startled than we were ourselves.

Our waggon loads of coal from Corfe avoided the sharp turning into the back drive by using a rough track from the top of the Knap, along the West Mead hedge.

It paid to buy a truck-load at a time and share it out. Between the wars best household coal could be had for thirty-five shillings a ton, with a small charge for delivery.

The cottage at the seaward end of the Rookery Wood was built by great-uncle John, and in his time was occupied by the head gardener. Subsequent gardeners, or perhaps their wives, preferred life in the village and so did the earlier coachmen. In consequence the house stood vacant for a while and my father allowed us to arrange our natural history collections in the empty rooms. From this the house acquired its name of Museum Cottage. It made a home for my brother and his wife for a little while when the House was occupied by W.A A.F's and before the evacuation. It faced due south with a view of hill and West Plantation. The front door, in an angle of the building, was so sheltered from the sea that delicate and half hardy plants grew on the walls beside it.

My elder sister, while the cottage was unoccupied, kept fowls there, housing them in the ample woodshed at the back. She sometimes fagged her juniors to go down and shut them in at night, a task we did not relish much on stormy evenings.

A tiger once escaped from a menagerie at Weymouth and was reputed to have killed a sheep near Osmington. That evening we were most reluctant to go through the shadowy wood, but our fears received no sympathy from our Spartan parents.

The last of the coachman to inhabit the Museum was Frederick Knight, its occupant for over fourteen years. He sadly brought the brougham and pair out for the last time on my wedding day, a month or so before the shadows of the first World War descended on the country One of the pair, then pensioned off with an unsound leg, was fetched from grass-fed idleness and worked upon with so much spit and polish that he became a fit companion for his elderly stable-mate. A photograph was taken of the carriage and pair on that occasion, so smart and pleasing to the eye that one can only feel regret for its passing off the stage with all the others of its kind. The gleaming coachwork, painted in dark green enamel with the "vleein' horse" in his heraldic colours on the panel of the door, the horses shining, every inch of them, from crest to toe, leather and metal polished to the last degree, and Knight himself, slim and upright on the box in his well-cut black cloth coat, white gloves and breeches, glossy boots, mahogany topped, and tall cockaded hat, make up a satisfying picture. Small details such as the pipe-clayed whiplash, well laid manes and carefully

oiled hooves, the glittering livery buttons and hat throwing back the
light, are evidence of the pride a coachman took in his calling and of
the trouble he was ready to take in order that his turn-out might appear
in tip-top trim.

Now that such objects have become a thing of the past it possibly
may be of interest to some to record that only army officers' servants
were entitled to cockaded hats, just as the balls surmounting pillars at
the entrance gates denoted officers' houses, and braid on evening
trousers was a mark of the same profession. The two last customs have
long lost their meaning, like the Old Etonian badge of the lowest
waistcoat button unfastened, flatteringly imitated, nowadays, by the
world at large.

I believe our station brougham had cost £150. It was built to last
for generations and would not soon become old-fashioned as does the
petrol-driven car. It rarely needed renovation or repair—(the brough-
ham was only once repainted in its lifetime) and sets of harness, reason-
ably cared for, wore for many years. A sound young horse could be
bought for £50 to £60 and he went on earning his keep for some ten
to a dozen years. He was seldom sick and had no tyres to puncture (a
set of new shoes meant a very small outlay then) nor did he make any
fuss over starting on frosty mornings. The greater part of his food and
all his bedding came off the estate, and the bedding went back to enrich
the land. So that to "keep a carriage and pair" though to the popular
mind a sign of affluence, compared to advantage with the cost of a car
and its upkeep.

But a coachman's life was a good deal harder than a chauffeur's.
He drove from an unsheltered seat, exposed to wind and weather and,
though wet, cold and tired at the end of the journey, must feed, water,
clean, and bed down his two horses before he could seek his own fire-
side and meal.

Only the youngest of Knight's children was born at the Museum
but the other three were very young when they came to Tyneham and
it was the only home they could remember. The elder girl has often
spoken to me of her happy childhood memories, her consolation in the
troubles of her later life.

Without the ready-made amusements children can enjoy to-day the
Tyneham boys and girls apparently led happy lives and entered into
home-made games with the utmost zest. The older boys spent time out
of school with their fathers in the fields or "helping" at the farm, with
pride at being associated with the occupations of the men. Certainly
simpler pleasures satisfied us all in those unsophisticated days. Some
pampered children of the vulgar rich possessed expensive toys and
boasted of them, as children of the vulgar rich in various walks of life
still do, but how we pitied them for being unable to invent original
and far more entertaining pastimes for themselves.

CHAPTER VIII

Tyneham Farm

AS long as my father kept the farm in hand it made a fascinating playground, full of friendly faces, animal as well as human.

The Tizzard family, such of them as were left at home, composed the backbone of the staff of workers on the farm. Alfred, the eldest, helped his father with the hedging and ditching and with the carpentry of the estate. William and George were carters and Charlie carters' boy. One sister, Mrs. Pitman, kept the post office and shop and another was her father's housekeeper. They represented a fine type of Dorset worker and had their sterling character written in their candid faces. The old man was a good though prejudiced craftsman, a martinet who ruled his family with a rod of iron. He made the gates and bars for the estate and he and Alfred often occupied the sawpit at the House, cutting out posts and planks with a cross-cut saw.

The barways which abounded in the valley and were so characteristic of the Purbeck scene were admirably suited to their place and purpose. Their solid 'posts', shaped from the local stone and weighing many hundredweight, were practically indestructible and needed no repairs, though now and again a post might settle out of plumb and need to be resunk. The planks which formed the cross-bars, always three in number, fitted the vertical slots cut into the posts and easily slipped in and out. To let sheep through, the lowest bar alone was moved. Horses and cattle stepped over the lowest when one end of the upper bars was dropped, and only for the passage of a waggon were all three removed. Our donkey made no bones about jumping all but the topmost bar. Barways possessed a great advantage over gates in having neither hinge nor catch to get out of order. Nor did they run the risk of being left unfastened inadvertently as a gate might easily be, to swing in the wind or yield to the pushing of an animal.

Most of the Tizzard brothers left the country when the farm was let, and crossed the seas to try their luck in Canada. George, who had married Louie Milsome, the adopted daughter of the schoolmistress, Mrs. Fry, very soon made good and started farming on his own, but tragedy and misfortune followed him and he and his wife both died comparatively young. Louie had been the monitress in Tyneham School, a gentle delicate girl afraid of a mouse. In Saskatchewan she became a model settler's wife, facing the heavy work and hardships with the utmost gallantry and tackling emergencies with brave determination. I hope that some of George and Louie's children are alive

79

and carrying on their parents' admirable qualities. Good-looking Bill has long since left this world and it is many years since I had news of Charlie. Of Alfred more anon.

The Tyneham farmstead was arranged in a series of closed-in yards stretching east and west. First, from the House end, came the rick-yard entered from the second Eweleaze. Through the warm rows of stacks one passed into the stableyard and was immediately confronted by the great barn doors on its further side. The carthorse stables shut the yard in on the right, with a long granary above them reached by an outside stair of stone at the eastern end. Along the granary floor stood the lines of corn bins, deep enough to bury a standing child in the heaped-up grain Each kind of corn had a different feel to the hand plunged down into the bin and each made a different whispering sound as the smoothly sliding grains slipped through the fingers or flowed back from sides to middle of the bin when a measureful was scooped from it.

The dogs adored the granary for it teemed with mice. The rats and mice had runs along the heading of the wall where it met the roof and we found that by rattling a stick along their runway we could persuade the mice to leave it for the floor, where the dogs despatched them in a trice.

The stable was designed for half a dozen horses, the number needed for the working of the farm. They were well cared for by the brothers Tizzard and were snugly stabled, though the building might not satisfy a present-day inspector. My father, with his long experience of horses, held that while in the stable carthorses should rest and that they needed warmth and darkness for their sleep He fully endorsed the comment of a Yorkshire brother-in-law who, when his cowstalls were officially declared to have too small windows mildly rejoined : "But *my* cows don't take in the evening paper".

The horses bore the traditional names associated with farm teams by immemorial usage. We might select what we thought suitable as a title for a newcomer, the carters just ignored our choice and named the new horse : "Blossom", "Captain", "Violet", "Duchess", "Bud" or "Queen", as the case might be.

On days when the waggons were to go to town the men would be in the stables from the early hours, watering, feeding and dressing up their teams. They took great pride in the horses' ornaments, which were the carters' personal possessions, and rubbed the brasses till they shone like gold. The manes and tails were plaited up with straw and coloured ribbons, hooves oiled and feathered heels combed out, washed, brushed and powdered. The horses' coats were rubbed and polished until they reflected every gleam of light. The teams were groomed as thoroughly as were the carriage horses and smelt as clean and good. Their carters vied with horse men from the neighbouring estates in smartness of turn-out, and what a heartening sight it was when the brightly painted waggons, drawn by their teams of gaily decorated and beribboned horses, took the road.

The waggon builders, too, were masters of their craft and the best of them built waggons of enduring beauty, with lines as clean and graceful as a ship's. The name of its maker was displayed conspicuously on the tail board of the waggon, whereas the owner's name and address hid modestly in smaller lettering on one side. The country lanes are poorer since the disappearance of those goodly sights and the cheerful chiming of the horse-bells, symbols of men's pride and satisfaction in their service to the land.

Across the yard from the stables stood the cartsheds, housing waggons, putts, rake, harrow, roller, hay tedder and all the other implements required on a farm in pre-mechanical days.

Between them and the rickyard wall the monster Devon bull resided in a spacious house with an outside pen where he could take the sun and air. The top flat of his dwelling was the hen-house, entered by a stairway from the Eweleaze.

The barn divided stable-yard and cow-yard, connected by the little pond-yard to the north. This last had a gate into the Cowleaze, which formed the main approach to the farmstead.

My father let us use the barn for our plays and pantomimes when we were raising money to build a village hall. He built a rough stage for us in the northern bay, with a professional slope and high enough at the back to allow for dressing room and property store below the platform.

One of our butlers who, in a "previous incarnation", had worked as stage hand in a Liverpool theatre, made us four sets of scenery and these, repainted over and over again, appeared in our successive entertainments.

The audience was accommodated in the long south bay, seating about 160 people comfortably.

The chairs we were obliged to hire from the Oddfellows' Hall in Wareham, whence the waggons fetched them. After the farm was let the tenant, Mr. Walter Smith, with commendable public spirit, lent us the barn for occasional entertainments, putting his men at our disposal for the necessary preparations, and the Tyneham Theatre only came to an end with the outbreak of the 1914 war.

The audiences were drawn from distances considerable in those days of slower transport, Blandford, Spetisbury, Sturminster Marshall, Wimborne and Parkstone sent contingents and Dorchester people made up chars-a-banc parties for the pantomimes.

The cowyard lying behind the barn was lined on two sides by the tie-up stalls, roofed over and with six-foot screens of furze, packed tight between posts, behind the cows. The Devon cattle throve in their airy winter bedrooms and were free from epidemics. At that time turning dairy cattle out on winter nights was thought to be the height of cruelty and wasteful farming.

A calf house with its back to the cow-yard faced the sun. Then came the piggeries, standing round a paved yard of their own, and last of all the sixth or dairy yard, adjoining dairy-house and dairy.

The dairyman's house and farmhouse formed one block of building with a common roof, excellent dwellings both. A colonnaded lean-to on the north side of the dairy-house accommodated the great cheese-press and the vats connected with the cheese-making, a process carried out by 'dairy chap' and wife in spotless pinners.

The Hulls were tenants of both Baltington and Tyneham farms for many years, Joseph at Tyneham and his brother James at Baltington. They were successful farmers and had charming families. By the time I was old enough to take some note of Tyneham people the farm was in the hands of Miss Hester Mary Hull who was living alone at Tyneham and soon to depart herself. I have some pleasant memories of her kindness to us children, asking us into her parlour as we passed on the way to the sea and giving us crisp and sugar-topped mixed biscuits.

James Hull later rented Higher Kingston Farm, near Dorchester and, after his death, his gifted daughter, Rosa Beatrice, lived to a good old age in the county town. With her the traditional friendship of our families was happily maintained until her death in 1954.

The top floor of the dairy house was all one airy room whose well-scrubbed boards were covered by rows of big blue vinny cheeses, in different stages of the ripening process. After the farm was let no more were made, but nothing could eradicate their penetrating smell.

The bailiff's "odd horse" stable and the spring-cart house lay west of the village-to-Worbarrow road where it joined the road from the House. A gate in the dip beside it, separating Ewe and Cow Leazes, marked where the road to the Bay became a private one. After the Admiralty had closed the Worbarrow Coastguard station they had renounced their right-of-way and the cost of keeping up the road devolved on the estate.

From the gate a short steep pitch ascended to the top of a Knap, where visitors' cars were parked in the years between the wars. The rapid increase in the number of these cars became a problem only to be solved by the closing of the last half mile of the road to all wheeled traffic unconnected with the Worbarrow population. The road was far too narrow to allow of vehicles passing one another and there was parking room for half a dozen cars at most at the top of the cliff. Nor was the road itself constructed to stand up to constant motor traffic and my father's means were insufficient either to make it so or to keep it in suitable repair. A very small number of visitors grumbled at being asked to walk the last few hundred yards. On the other hand there were many who expressed their gratitude for the prohibition which kept Worbarrow peaceful and unspoilt, in contrast to the noise and overcrowding of so many other bays along the coast.

Before my brother was deprived of Tyneham he was pondering ways and means of levelling some ground to give more parking space at Worbarrow, while making access to it safer for the lighter kind of traffic.

The parish could not furnish level ground enough to make a cricket pitch. Play was attempted once or twice at the foot of the South Hill opposite the farm, but odds against it were too great. Football was equally unplayable, though I remember men and boys attempting to practice in the triangle of the Cowleaze which had Toadstile for its apex.

A public footpath from the village crossed the stream below the village pond, kept close to the hedge of the "Leg" and made its way through the Gwyle to the Worbarrow road at Toadstile. Here wickets at either side of the strip of woodland gave on to steep descents of large flat stones, embedded in the banks to form a stairway. The path was over-arched by hazel and, on passing through the gates, the walker stepped at once from daylight into a cool dark shade, needing a moment to adjust his vision to the change. His nose was gratefully assailed by the fresh, "green", watery smell of harts'-tongue ferns, a scent unlike any other known to me. The pathway crossed the miniature ravine on a flat stone bridge. No toads, to my knowledge, lived in Toadstile and it is possible that the name derived from an earlier right-of-way referred to as "t'owd stile".

From Toadstile onwards to the sea the Gwyle stream formed the boundary between the Grange and Tyneham properties and, as it cut the covert in two throughout its length, the shooting of it was a joint affair between the families. It was the custom to begin the day at Way-ground withy-beds and work through Limekiln, Long Coppice, Rook Grove and the withy-beds at Baltington before beginning on the Gwyle. The Grange and Tyneham gamekeepers and beaters worked together amicably, though Henry Miller firmly stood by his right of giving the orders while on Tyneham territory. Henry contrasted picturesquely with the orthodox appearance of the visitors from Grange, in his much-worn, shapeless velveteens, their pockets bulged with furred and feathered game, his home-knit fishing "garnsey" in thick navy blue, and his billycock hat, once black but long since changed to green by the salty winds. Henry directed guns to stations "fore" and "aft", and strangers to the Dorset language found his speech as difficult to understand as double Dutch.

Those shooting days in long-past Christmas holidays stand out among my happiest memories. To be out in the open all day long in Tyneham woods and fields was bliss enough, and added to this was the pleasure of being in company with friends ; guns, keepers, beaters, stops and dogs. The evident enjoyment of them all, the cheerful, often witty comments of the beaters, the animal, bird and insect life to be watched at leisure as one waited "forward", the exercise of beating and retrieving, all combined to make the day a time of unalloyed content-ment. Our guests were entertained by the beaters' use of compass points to warn the guns, as cries of : "Bunny going west!" "A-a-h ! a girt heäre coming north !" and so forth echoed through the woods, accompanied by Henry's voice encouraging the men to "rottle up they sticks". Black rabbits, not unusual then, were known as "pa'sons" and were spared by common consent. I call to mind a ferreting occasion when a rabbit had laid up and caused a deal of trouble. It was at last dug out after strenuous labour and much wasted time. Henry's great paw was thrust into the hole and clutched a little rabbit some six inches long. Holding the wretched victim out at arm's length Henry shook his head and said, reproachfully and sadly : "You-girt-*coward* !"

Another chance remark of his has stuck in my mind, though many wittier ones have long since been forgotten. It was in the South African war and a tale was going round that an angelic visitant had promised President Kruger victory for his cause. Henry, commenting on this, said drily : "I d'low thic eängel had a black veäce".

We always came back to the House for luncheon on our shooting days and the beaters had theirs, with a flagon of beer, by the Old House open hearth. The bag was usually a very modest one but gave a day's amusement shared by everyone concerned. A typical day produced some thirty to forty pheasants, perhaps a hundred rabbits, half a dozen hares, a woodcock and some "miscellaneous". Roedeer were sometimes seen but always spared.

The game was laid out at the end of the day on the raised stone walk by the Old House door. After the beaters had received their share the rest was hung in the dairy, to be sent next day to Wareham market.

Walking up partridges was another pleasant occupation for the young and energetic, involving heavy going through the furze and roots and endless scrambling up and down the hills. The coveys had an aggravating trick of rising on one hill and swinging right across the valley to the opposite side, returning, well out of shot, to their original starting-place as soon as the guns had followed them across the ups and downs of the valley floor. The joy of being out in the September sunshine amply compensated for the smallness of the bag.

We children learned to shoot with a double-barrelled "collector" a beautiful little gun and light to handle. When we had "passed" to my father's satisfaction with the .410 we were promoted to a single-barrelled 16-bore. My father, usually so lenient with his children, was rigorously, not to say fiercely, strict about the handling of guns and came down heavily upon the slightest sign of carelessness. Once having roused his anger by some thoughtless conduct with a gun we never risked incurring it again. Visiting guns who failed to unload when crossing fence or ditch or who "followed on" were seldom asked again.

The harvesting of hay and corn crops took place far later in the season then than now, and there was generally a breathing space for man and horse between the end of haysel and the start of corn harvest. I can remember mowing and reaping still being done with scythe and

TYNEHAM FARM

sickle, but soon the horse-drawn mowing and reaping machines had
superseded hand work. Even so the scytheman played his part by cutting
a passage round the field for the mowing-machine.

Haymaking was a leisurely affair compared with its modern counterpart and the June weeks when the valley air was heavy with the fragrance of the drying grass were to my mind the high light of the summer.
Haysel was ushered in by the bright sound of whetstones on the
scythe blades. Then the machine began its steady whirring, like the
nightjars' spinning-wheel note, broken at regular intervals by the
driver's musical cry : "Woa back!" and the click of the knife disen-
gaging as the horses were pulled up and backed for the turn at the
corner of the cut. Along with these cheerful sounds arose the intoxicating scent of fresh cut grass and flowers, a scent which subtly
changed with each day's processes until it became the ripe and sober
sweetness of the fully sun-dried hay. All hands were pressed into the
hayfield, first for the tossing and spreading of the swathes with forks,
then for the raking into narrow rows, to be assembled later into wind-
rows and, in uncertain weather, into cocks.

For women and children it was a delightful holiday, a welcome
excuse for being in the open air, with festive picnics in the shade of a
hedgerow tree, when mothers and grannies brought the dinners out to
spread upon the grass, bedding the babies down to sleep on heaps of
hay.

My mother tried, one year, to introduce the haytime drink so
popular on her brother's sheep run in New Zealand, sending out
gallons of oatmeal water to the fields, in jugsful for the men and
bucketsful for the horses, but though the horses relished it the men
stayed faithful to their bottles of cold tea. The "owls" of cider and
home-brewed beer no longer, sad to say, accompanied their owners to
the fields. My father could remember the good days when every
cottage had its pig, and home-cured bacon, whole-meal bread and
local cheeses formed the agricultural workers' staple diet, resulting in
clear complexions, sound white teeth and absence of digestive troubles,
these last already rife in the villages fifty years ago.

Corn harvest never held such magic for us children as the haying
time, partly because it mostly fell outside the summer holidays. By
the time that I first remember it the women folk had vanished from
the fields except for gleaning* when the waggon loads of corn had left
the fields. Then they would flock out to the stubbles with their sacks
and baskets and perambulators, gathering grain enough to keep their
chicken in hard food throughout the winter and wheat to grind and
bake for the family's bread. In my very early years a kindly farmer
neighbour used to fill the pockets of our reefer coats with wheat at
threshing-time to be ground to flour in the coffee-mill at home and
turned into grimy wholemeal scones for nursery tea. I only tasted

* "leäzen" to the Dorset born.

85

furmety on one occasion, when it made a strong appeal to my childish palate. I wonder whether, if I met it again, it would taste as good as memory suggests.

Besides being reaped much later then than now it seems to me that the corn remained far longer in the stook or stitch. My father often quoted the old saying that the "oats in stitch must hear the church bells ring three times before going home", implying that they were not fit to stack before three Sundays had passed by.

I never saw a "neck" or "corn dolly" at Tyneham, but the last waggon-load of harvest rumbled home accompanied by great hilarity and singing of old songs, together with shrill cheering on the children's part.

CHAPTER IX

The Village

THE seemly row of houses in the "street" is scheduled as of special interest and affords a good example of harmonious building with the local stone, topped up with kind stone tiles instead of merciless slate. The road was once divided from the gardens by a quickset hedge. In time the hedge became untidy and unsightly and my father cut it down, replacing it with a mortared wall of rough-dressed stone.

The lowest cottage in the row was the shepherd's by tradition and occupied for many years by the Lucas family. 'Shepherd' was silent and reserved and, like the great majority of his calling at that time, a conscientious and devoted servant of his flock, putting their welfare far before any comfort or convenience of his own.

His wife, who had been a Wilcox, must have been an outstandingly beautiful woman in her youth, and her tribe of fair and blue-eyed children all inherited her looks. As if her numerous offspring and their progeny were not enough to occupy her heart and hands she made herself the unofficial sick nurse of the village, dealing with accidents and confinements with remarkable skill.

My mother had the cause of district nursing much at heart. To her initiative and energy was due the founding of a cottage hospital and nursing service in and round the town of Fordingbridge and she would not rest until she had obtained a qualified nurse for the inhabitants of Tyneham, Povington and Grange. The first to undertake the work was a devoted woman who endeared herself to all her patients, in spite of the resentment and suspicion roused by something hitherto unknown. Nurse Gostling lived at Tyneham and went to and from her cases on a bicycle, by day and night, in every kind of weather, no light achievement in the then condition of the roads. The work became too much for her and it was obvious that to make the project workable a larger area must be served and a car provided for the nurse's use. The scheme presented very many difficulties but my mother was undefeated and eventually inaugurated the West Purbeck Nursing Association, with my younger sister as its honorary secretary, Church Knowle and Kimmeridge, with their outlying farms and cottages, being brought into the district served. Unfortunately there was little support except from a generous few including the small number of landowners concerned, and criticisms were more readily forthcoming than financial help. Prolonged and gallant efforts failed to keep the good work going and, to the great loss of the neighbourhood, the Association had to be closed down.

87

My mother took keen interest in the Red Cross Children's Hospital at Swanage and loved to visit it. In addition she was local secretary for the Soldiers' and Sailors' Families Association and the Royal United Kingdom Beneficent Association, both of which involved considerable correspondence.

To return to Tyneham Village. The shepherd's house was neighboured by the post office and shop. The Mores', mother and sons, were its occupants when I knew it first and one son was the village baker. Another worked as under-gardener at the House and a third, Jim, married our pretty housemaid Alice and with her worked a small heath farm at Povington. After the family moved from Tyneham there was no successor in the bakery, and bread thenceforward came from Corfe in Hibbs' van.

The Mores' were followed by Mrs. Pitman, one of the Tizzard sisters, postmistress for many years until she married Joseph Miller as his second wife. Her daughter, "Queenie" Pitman, married Basil, Joseph's son, the only male representative of his generation and last of the Worbarrow Millers.

The shop was a tempting place in Mrs. Pitman's reign. She always welcomed us and let us look consideringly at all her goods before deciding how to spend our precious pennies. The premises were tiny and one five-foot counter served both shop and post office, but every inch of window space and walls was crammed with wares, the heavier articles, such as boxes of lard and bags of flour and soda, standing on the floor.

Three customers at a time produced a traffic jam and, when the counter was piled high with parcels waiting for the postman, the postmistress was scarcely visible behind the rampart.

The shop had a fine, rich blend of smells, bacon and cheese predominating, with alluring under-currents of tea, liquorice and peppermint. There was a varied choice of biscuits to be had at popular prices. (I specially remember "butter creams", juicy and toothsome at three halfpence a quarter), and chocolate and sweets to suit all comers. Fry's chocolate cream was on sale in big, thick bars at a penny apiece and a penn'orth of sugared almonds, bulls' eyes, acid drops, fruit jellies and the like filled a sizeable bag. There were comfits, too, in different shapes and colours, bearing romantic legends :—"Will you be my sweetheart?" "I love you", "Will you be mine?" . . . and jars full of mammoth peppermint humbugs. Ha'porths were served just as willingly as were the larger amounts, and a fat bag of popcorn was sold for a farthing. In fact, a penny spelt riches when spent at the shop.

A big cardboard box displayed needles and thimbles, cotton reels, mending wool, buttons and tape, all priced at a copper or two. Another box held sundry stationery items, penny bottles of ink, double sheets of glossy white notepaper pleasant to write on, pens, pencils, sealing-wax, wrappers and gum.

Shoe laces, matches, lozenges, garden seeds and balls of string, oil, candles, blacking and vinegar crowded the corners.

The telephone, for the receipt and dispatch of telegrams only, lived in the kitchen for the sake of privacy, but Mrs. Pitman's voice repeating messages could be distinctly heard by customers in the shop. The substance of incoming telegrams was often known all round the village before they reached their lawful destination. Before the coast-guard were disbanded telegrams for Tyneham came through the Worbarrow station. Then and when later they were handled by the post office at Grange the charge to the recipient for delivery was sixpence, no account of distance being taken. A dozen words were telegraphed for sixpence with a halfpenny charge for each additional word.

The telephone did not reach the House until 1935, when it was put in prior to Dr. Sauer's tenancy.

When Mrs. Pitman married Joseph Miller in 1910 her place was taken by Mrs. Barnes (afterwards Mrs. Herd) who kept the post office and shop for many years and was succeeded by the last of the Tyneham postmistresses, Mrs. Driscoll.

According to Mrs. Lucas the shepherd's house and the post office had been 'rebuilt' (more probably restored and improved) about 1881, when the houses at the north end of the row were also altered. The roofs were raised and stone tiles took the place of the earlier thatch.

The house next door to the post office on the other side "went with" the farm and housed successive carters and farm labourers.

The school-house occupied the bend of the street and was connected by its garden to the school itself. As Tyneham church had neither tower nor spire the parish flagstaff stood in the school-house grounds and flew its flag on all ecclesiastical, national and local "occasions". A makeshift pole on the Knap between village and farm had served for Empire Days and other times of national rejoicing until my father gave the staff and had it planted safe from cattle in the school-house garden.

The first of the schoolma'ams I can call to mind is Mrs. Fry, who suffered from arthritis and was very lame but kept her charges in good order nevertheless. In course of time she followed her adopted daughter and the latter's husband out to Canada and was succeeded by Miss Woodman, an excellent and conscientious teacher, who cared for the moral and physical welfare of her charges as well as for their mental education.

She used to raise the wherewithal to buy potatoes and roasted them to form a hot accompaniment to the children's dinners. She also collected money for warm slippers to be worn in school, while boots and stockings dried by the central stove. She kept a watchful eye on her pupils' outfits and saw to it that the poorer mothers had some help in keeping families well clothed and shod.

Miss Woodman was, I am certain, typical of the good village teachers of her day. The children taught by them enjoyed a personal, sympathetic care based upon intimate knowledge of each scholar's background and his individual needs, a knowledge dependent upon teacher and taught being members of the same close-knit community.

Until the children were transferred to a central school, when Tyneham school was closed, they enjoyed complete immunity from epidemics.

A child in need of special treatment went to hospital or sanatorium on the strength of "letters" collected by my mother from subscribers to the various institutions.

Miss Woodman's love for the youngsters under her care was deep and totally unsentimental, accompanied by a firm belief in discipline. She gave her pupils high ideals and standards of behaviour, wholeheartedly believing that to build character and form good citizens was every teacher's foremost duty.

I can recall so many of Miss Woodman's scholars who have proved themselves to be of sterling worth and usefulness to the community. I cannot think of more than one or two exceptions who have betrayed her trust in them.

She did not believe in crowding and bewildering their young minds with a host of subjects likely to be useless to the great majority in after life, preferring a solid grounding in essentials for both boys and girls, to fit them for the lives ahead of them and for later specialisation.

It is hard to avoid comparison of letters written to me by her former pupils with the average compositions emanating from the schools of every grade to-day.

Old Tyneham scholars write in clear, distinctive hands, their letters abound with information and ideas both well and easily expressed and there are few erasures or mistakes in spelling.

Miss Woodman taught the children to be interested in their surroundings, in country things in general and in rural occupations. She was always ready to help them towards practical efficiency and many of her pupils must have blessed her, if not at the time then later on in life, for all the trouble she took over teaching them to "make and mend".

She was a competent organist and gave her scholars an example of devoted service to the Church.

The "street" curved round the schoolhouse garden into the schoolyard, where the school and the rectory cottages closed a cul-de-sac.

The school, erected by Nathaniel Bond of Grange about 1870, was a single room with a lobby at one end and, at the other, a platform for the infants' desks and benches.

Until the village hall materialised all local gatherings and entertainments had to take place in the school. I wonder, now, how we contrived to stage elaborate programmes on the narrow little platform, and how so many people crammed into the body of the room. It is true that the men and boys paid threepence for the privilege of occupying perches on the tops of bookcases or standing at the back, and somehow the remainder of the population squeezed itself into what space was left.

Before each entertainment the unwieldy forms with heavy iron frames were coaxed out through the lobby into the yard and stacked against a wall, protected by a rick sheet. Each household lent its chairs for the occasion and these, of every shape and kind, well chalked with their owner's names, arrived at the school some hours before the show, so that their public spirited owners stood to have their teas. After the concert came the sorting out of chairs, and the audience set off homewards carrying their property.

Sometimes the village got up a concert on its own, but I think this enterprise died out with the closing of the coastguard station.

Sometimes we worked up plays and dances with the children. The chief (perhaps only) merit of these entertainments was the fact that they were home-produced. As such they probably gave more pleasure to more people than any ready-made performance staged by "foreigners".

In the earlier, less sophisticated and less self-conscious days the parish discovered any amount of varied talent. Some of the singing voices, though untrained, were good, and there was plenty of humour ready to appear, though as a rule the singers liked their numbers in a grave and even melancholy vein, keeping the comic touch for recitations, duologues and sketches. The songs most often dwelt in mournful strains on tombs and partings, setting suns and weeping willows, to the apparent satisfaction of their hearers. Apart from this persistent liking for the dismal, the taste of the performers was not once at fault. I cannot call to mind a single lapse into coarse or dubious humour and once, when imported talent ventured on a quite innocuous breakdown on the stage, the village voiced its disapproval for a long while afterwards.

The children's plays were always a success, if not from the producer's at least from the spectators' point of view. Admiring families applauded the performers without prejudice or favour and the evening's entertainment ended in a riot of excitement, with the actors joining wildly in the cheers and clapping.

We came to know the schoolroom well through holding Sunday classes in it over many years. For a long time we three sisters taught the children in those classes, then, after my elder sister's marriage, one of our former scholars joined the "staff" and taught the infants.

Our qualifications were on the slender side, our knowledge of teaching nil and our methods would, I am sure, appal the highly trained instructor of more scientific times. I scarcely dare confess to the amount of memorising that we made the children do in the hope that at least some small proportion of the teaching might remain with them.

The Tyneham children as a whole were slow in learning but, once mastered, anything they learned stuck in their minds, as I know from their own acknowledgments in after years. I have heard with thankfulness how psalms and collects lingered in their memories and gave them words in which to voice their faith and seek for comfort in their troubles.

Long after I had ceased to teach the Tyneham boys and girls I learned from London parish priests how often the ancient prayers and hymns once memorised in childhood returned to the surface in the hours of stress and were the one link with religion still remaining in a slum dweller's mind. The once familiar words repeated to the dying have struck an answering chord again and again when other approaches have been powerless to help.

And so I remain impenitent for having given the children truths to possess and hold by such archaic methods.

The school served as a reading-room on winter evenings and the lads could borrow books there or play table games.

A gate into the laundry garden occupied the south-west corner of the yard. Both laundry cottages faced south, so that the stone-flagged walk before their doors and the two deep porches made the most of the sun. Theirs was the pleasantest position in the village, warm and sheltered, close to church and street but not too crowded by the neighbours. The first one made a refuge for my brother and his wife when they were evicted from the House and before the Museum Cottage was made ready to receive them. A narrow "leg" between the garden and Mount Mead broke the full violence of the south-west winds and made a cool retreat in summer.

Here Mrs. Taylor reigned for many years, a cheerful bustling soul with a genial word for everyone she met and an infectious laugh. She ran the laundry, coped efficiently with her family and was official caretaker to the church and school as well.

The rectory cottages, a very ancient building, filled the west side of the yard. They served as rectory before Nathaniel Bond, the builder of the school, replaced them by the present parsonage some eighty years ago. In our time they were separate cottages, the lower one inhabited by Henry Charles, a pensioner of the rector, Mr. Homan; the other lent or let to summer visitors and sometimes lived in by the rector himself during summer holidays when tenants occupied the rectory. There was a tiny knot garden beneath the windows, fenced from the school yard by a low stone wall and patterned out in little formal flower-beds neatly edged with box.

Some steps ascended from this plot to the Rectory garden, a big rectangular enclosure bounded on one side by the churchyard wall and shielded to the northward by a row of pollarded elms. The garden was prolific, with a rich, warm soil and, though less sheltered than the kitchen garden at the House, its crops matured much earlier. Baskets of roses, asparagus and strawberries arrived as presents from the rectory a week or two before the House could gather any of its own.

A myrtle, grown from a sprig in the wedding bouquet of Mrs. Homan's sister, stood in the open centre of the garden, six feet high and flowering profusely every year.

The grove of trees which closed the garden to the west had long been used as a burial place for rectory pets and was described by an earlier rector's wife, an Irish great-great-aunt of ours, as being "alive with dead dogs".

My husband's grandfather, Nathaniel Bond of Grange, who built the rectory on succeeding to the property, was patron of the living and its holder too. During his long incumbency his brother-in-law, the Reverend William Truell, served as his curate and was resident at Tyneham. The parson's wife and the curate's were twin Hawkesworth sisters. Another assistant priest was housed at Steeple in the latter years of "Uncle Nat's" long life.

The rectory, a plain and an unassuming building, with a cheerful air of modest comfort, could accommodate a typical Victorian family. Canon Christopher Wordsworth's olive branches numbered nine. The living was reckoned a good one but required a rector with some private income of his own. The Wordsworth budget would not run to carriage or trap, so Mrs. Wordsworth regularly walked the dozen miles to Wareham and back for household shopping, as did all Tyneham housewives, returning with perambulators heaped with merchandise on top of babies. We hear so much of the lower standard of living "before the wars", but in spite of it the country people must have been a good deal hardier and stronger than their grandchildren.

No carrier ever plied from Tyneham and, for the carriage of their heavier goods, the inhabitants depended on the journeys of farm waggons into town, or the kind offices of anyone who owned a horse and cart.

During the 1914-18 war my sister did the village shopping with her four-wheeled dog-cart, summer and winter and in every type of weather.

Parcels for farms and cottages reached by field tracks were deposited by the road to "wait till called for". I can remember being told in a history lesson that, in Alfred's reign, a woman wearing all her jewellery and carrying gold could walk alone from end to end of England safe from molestation, and I wondered why the chronicler considered it worth recording. It certainly never crossed our minds that there could be any risk in leaving valuable parcels unattended by the public way.

The front door of the rectory faced east and the gravelled square before it had a screen of evergreen oaks. The entrance gate originally stood between the grove of ilex and the kitchen garden. My father leased to the incumbent a triangular piece of land, at a peppercorn rent of one red rose a year, to extend the approach and keep the cattle further from the house. The gate was then moved out to the apex of the triangle, close to the churchyard wall. The rector of the time laid out the additional plot as an orchard and backed the ilexes with a belt of deciduous trees, making a little water garden by the stream and planting flowering shrubs along the drive.

The rectory probably enjoyed more hours of sunshine than any other dwelling in the parish and paid for its open site by its exposure to the wind. It was unfortunate that Canon Wordsworth, arriving in the summer, objected to the stand of fir trees planted on the Mount to form a windbreak, on the ground that they spoilt the perfect view of the sea. He felled the trees forthwith and he and his successors never ceased to regret his hasty action. In spite of solid walls and double windows gales were often terrifying to the occupants of the house. One rector, when the wind was high, betook himself with lamp and books to the empty cellar and wore the night out there to the thunder of the gusts. My kinswoman, Mrs. Truell, is said to have called for brandy and her Bible in a similar crisis, but this is perhaps apocryphal.

The Reverend C. S. Homan followed Canon Wordsworth in the living in 1897 and stayed at Tyneham nearly seventeen years. He and his wife, May Digby of Studland Manor, were very kind to us when we were children and in and out of the rectory almost every day. Their boys, both killed in the first World War, were a good deal younger than ourselves.

In the early part of Mr. Homan's rectorate, the Reverend William Filliter was his assistant priest and lived at Steeple rectory. They served, between them, the four churches, several miles apart, of Steeple, Tyneham, Grange and Holme, aided by pony-carts and bicycles. Later the charge of Holme was taken over by the rector of East Stoke and for many years Mr. Homan served the remaining churches single-handed, at first depending on his bicycle for transport. Then, when he found the hilly journeys too exhausting, especially in wet or windy weather, he taught himself to ride and thenceforth did his travelling on horseback.

My father's grandfather had added a considerable sum to the endowment on condition that the church at Tyneham was provided with two services, complete with sermon, every Sunday, a complication of the incumbent's duties. It meant five services in widely scattered churches and, as a rule, two crossings of the hill, with sandwich meals to be eaten on the march or in the vestries. This most exacting obligation was fulfilled for many years by Mr. Homan, in addition to long daily visiting rounds on foot, in the course of which he rendered practical as well as spiritual aid to the sick and aged, turning his competent hand to any job which needed doing in the isolated cottages.

The rectory had stabling for three, a couple of good grass fields above the house, and a slice of the hill, sandwiched between the Grange and Tyneham lands. Mount Mead, in front of the house, had cowsheds sheltering under the "Mount", where a small pit yielded gravel and sand. Here ancient human remains were exhumed from time to time, with Samian ware and Kimmeridge "coal money", the two last being found in many other places in the parish.

The rectory roof was built with too shallow a pitch, giving rise to perpetual trouble. The rain poured into the house after storms and hundreds of pounds were spent on repairs with no lasting improvement; in fact the state of the Rectory Roof became our perennial nightmare. We worked to raise the money to pay off the builders and, just as we thought ourselves clear and our energies free to be turned into some more rewarding channel, the cry would go up that the roof had sprung a new leak. I think that not less than a thousand pounds was spent on repairs and attempts to improve the conditions.

At the top of the Village street the tap of spring water from Madmore stood back in a stone-built recess with a trough for the overflow and a stone slab for the resting of pails. At the back of the niche words from the fourth chapter of S. John were cut into the stone : "Whosoever drinketh of this water shall thirst again, but whosoever drinketh of the water that I shall give him shall never thirst".

The pollarded trunk of a great elm stood guard over the tap and formed the notice-board for local events. To one side of it an oak tree, planted to commemorate the coronation of King George the Fifth, grew in a grass plot shielded by an iron cage.

The top of the street was closed by a gate across the Lulworth road. A wicket gate alongside and a metalled pathway led to the head gardener's cottage, passing the backs of two more houses on the way. These houses were both small and inconvenient, the only poor ones in the village and only suitable for housing one or at most two persons. The eastern cottage was long occupied by old George Richards and, when he could no longer "do for himself", by a widowed sister who looked after him.

The other cottage held the Alfred Tizzards, who would have managed well in it by themselves but had Mrs. Tizzard's invalid and crippled brother, Philip Harvell, living with them and were seldom without a brother's or sister's child as well. For such a number the one living-room was far too small, the stairs were steep and awkward for the sick man and the bedroom space inadequate. My father had no other house available and, for poor Philip's sake, he shut his eyes to the overcrowding which he disapproved.

95

In spite of the congestion the small living room was bright and cosy and Mrs. Tizzard made a happy home of it. I had a deep affection for her, more than for any of the other Tyneham friends, and spent many hours with her and Phil. Both were as good as gold, affectionate and gentle, bearing their troubles with no murmur of complaint. Poor Philip was brought down by Alfred, every morning, with the help of a neighbour or of Mr. Homan, and set in an armchair by the fire where he stayed for the rest of the day, reading a little but mostly looking out of the window and across the valley to the hill. I never once saw Phil impatient and his sister was as gallant as himself both then and when in later life she too became quite helpless. They spoke in the soft sing-song Dorset manner and to be in their company was to experience peace and serenity. Some of my earliest contacts with true saintliness I owe to them and, in my long life, have met few to equal those two friends and the others sharing the same quality in the neighbourhood of Tyneham.

On looking back I now see what a source of strength and sure support they possessed in their religion. It gave them a foundation like a rock on which to build a peace which no exterior affliction could shatter or shake. They lacked material comforts and the many advantages daily taken for granted by their grandchildren. Their lives on the physical plane were often unspeakably hard, but their steady faith transcended all the troubles and hardships of this world and gave to them a spring of comfort close at hand and never failing. They lived in the knowledge that all pain is passing but that goodness shall endure and in the certain hope of the promised vision and reward awaiting the faithful servant's homecoming at the long day's end. The knowledge was written for all to see in their cheerful, happy faces.

It is hard to express my thankfulness for the truths these noble men and women taught me and I never think of my unconscious teachers save with reverence and affection.

One of my treasured possessions is a Staffordshire jug, long handed down from mother to daughter in Mrs. Tizzard's family. She had intended me to have it at her death but gave it to me in her lifetime.

After Phil's death the Tizzards moved away from Tyneham and it was many years before we met again at Puddletown. By that time she was bedridden and totally dependent upon Alfred's gentle ministrations. He nursed and tended her devotedly and, in a tiny, inconvenient house, she looked as perfectly cared for as she might have done in a well-staffed hospital ward. She was as patient and as bright as ever in her helpless and monotonous existence. Asked if a wireless set would give her pleasure her face lit up like that of a delighted and excited child but she did not live to see the set installed, dying a few days later just as quietly and unobtrusively as she had lived.

The last house on the east side of the Village was the gardener's, another of Uncle John's additions, built on the same plan as the

Museum Cottage but with no entrance at the back. This was intended to eliminate draughts from opposite outer doors but, rather naturally, was not appreciated by the housewives who inhabited the house.

In the North Cowleaze, just above the gardener's cottage, stood the village hall. The modest structure represented many years of effort in the shape of fêtes, sales, concerts, competitions and the like. It was not until October 1924 that it was formally opened. The hut, which comfortably held the whole community, cost, with its chairs and other furnishings, two hundred pounds. And five years later it was totally destroyed in the tremendous gale of December 1929. The hut was torn from its foundations and completely wrecked. Sections of roof, some of which half a dozen men could scarcely lift, were wafted over the belt of trees between the Cowleazes, a lamp chimney with unbroken glass was picked up later on the hill top near Spring Gate and portions of wings and flies were carried by the wind to Three Acres, where the high hedge caught and held them. The piano travelled a considerable distance before settling in a pool of water.

It was some years before the hut's successor rose upon the derelict site.

In this terrible gale, beginning on the fourth day of December and raging for five days and nights without a pause, some fifty trees fell round about the House and many more were smashed or thrown upon their neighbours. Three of them fell together from the Rookery Wood into the flower garden, crushing a number of ornamental shrubs and breaking the old sycamores, where owls had always nested. An elm crashed from the Avenue into the second garden, without, however, damaging the wall.

Another huge elm and a silver fir came down across the stable plot, and most of the silvers in the West Plantation and Great Wood were either thrown or split in two. The ancient yew between the drive gate and the north-east corner of the House was one of the victims, though it fell up-wind. Both back drive and sea road were blocked by fallen trees and many pines in the "New Forest" were uprooted. Three limes which crashed together, halfway up the Avenue, righted themselves when sawn through at a height of twelve feet from the ground.

Most of the trees in the Eweleaze group above the garden gate into the Rookery Wood were lost, including a fine service tree. Damage to smaller trees and bushes was past computation. The laurels in the Rookery Wood were blackened and stripped of many of their leaves.

Farm, cottages and outbuildings lost quantities of tiles and a stone tile from the House roof fell through the skylight in the passage to the dining room.

Returning down the village street and passing between the shepherd's house and pond one came by a grassy track and field gate to the Gwyle Cottages, built about 1880 of local stone with stone-tiled roofs to match the "street". They stood in an enclosure of their own and faced the Gwyle.

CHAPTER X
The Church

I have kept the church to the last, although it was the first thing to attract attention in the village scene and was the centre of the small community in more ways than one. It stood on sloping ground and the site on the village side had been artificially raised to make a level grave-yard so that its turf, within a strong retaining wall, was five or six feet higher than the street. The building's ancient history and architectural points are well described in Hutchins' *History of Dorset*.

My father's grandfather had added the South transept when the seating in the church became inadequate and the north transept, until then the family pew, was given over to the congregation. The family vault is under the south transept, but my father's and his mother's graves are in the churchyard by the transept door. When my mother died in 1949 the church and churchyard were already derelict and she is buried in the cemetery at Dorchester instead of with my father.

The transept was divided from the body of the church by a low oak screen and door*. A crudely coloured window to the memory of my great-aunt Mary filled the southern wall and three stained glass lights by Powell lit the transept from the east†.

The oaken bosses of the coffered roof were carved with shields emblazoned with armorial bearings. Three Caen stone monuments on the inner wall commemorated my great-grandparents and their sons and daughters.

The instant that one stepped inside the transept door one met the enchanting smell of an ancient village church unbaked by central heating and unspoilt by leaking gas. The smell was three parts mould and leather bindings, laced with a mixture of old music books, straw hassocks, candle-wax and lamp oil.

The stove, a "Tortoise" bearing on its lid the appropriate legend: "Slow but sure combustion", fitted an angle of the arches at the crossing and diffused a grateful heat. When it was going strong the church felt like what the cookery books described as "a moderate

---

* These and the Jacobean pulpit are now, I believe, on loan to Lulworth Camp.
† These lights portrayed a figure of Fortitude in armour, supported by two angels, in commemoration of my elder brother's gallant and triumphant fight with pain, from the siege of Ladysmith in 1899 until his death, at the age of thirty-one, in 1911.

oven". The lamps, too, helped to keep the congregation snug on Sunday evenings. Five powerful double burners swinging from the ceiling threw out a pleasant blaze of yellow light to welcome worshippers from the dark and cold. My father vetoed the suspension of a lamp from the south transept roof and the family pews depended for illumination on two bracket lamps with tin reflectors, one on each window ledge. They stood at somewhere about shoulder level and only the books of the nearest worshippers received their light, so it was just as well to know the hymns and evening psalms by heart.

As soon as we reached our 'teens we joined the choir and sat with the other songsters in the chancel. The sounds emitted by the vocalists made up in volume what they lacked in pitch and concord. Our efforts, if not harmonious, were at any rate wholehearted and probably as efficacious as the more genteel and musical expression of our brethren in the towns. We were not unduly critical of our neighbours' contributions but doggedly held on our individual ways through chant and hymn, together offering up a loud and cheerful noise.

New words and tunes were coldly looked upon and it was long before they took their places in the popular esteem, but the old familiar favourites were sure of being rendered with the utmost heartiness however often we might sing them.

In the north transept, once the family pew, a Williams monument adorned the wall. We came to know its satisfying shape and bright heraldic colours well, from facing it through many sermon times.

Near it a little stained-glass roundel, set in the mullioned window to the west, pictured Our Lady and the Holy Child, with the encircling motto: "*Il nay autre*", sadly defaced by time and weather. This little gem, brought back from Flanders by a member of the family, has now been wantonly broken up if not destroyed.

A homely feature of the transept and of the wall beneath the gallery at the west end of the church was a row of hat-pegs freely used in service time. This sensible arrangement never struck us as peculiar until it caused amusement to a visiting party of archaeologists from Bournemouth.

Elizabeth Tarrant's monument was built into the north wall of the nave, with the following inscription :—

"Near this place lyes the body of Elizabeth Tarrant,
servant to Mrs. Bond of Tyneham, in which station
she continued 34 yeares.
To the memory of her Prudence, Honesty and
Industry this monument is erected.
She died August ye 2nd 1769 in the 54 yeare
of her age."

Under it hung the framed and painted panel to the memory of Hannah Hurworth, designed and carried out by Lawrence Turner and setting forth her 46 years of devoted service, together with the love and honour in which she was held.

Above, on the front of the gallery, hung a much older panel in a black wood frame, bearing the words :—
"O worship the Lord in the beauty of holiness"
in eighteenth century lettering, black on white.

The chancel held the organ given by my parents as a thankoffering for my brother's homecoming, maimed but miraculously safe, from the siege of Ladysmith. The little instrument, by Burton Brothers of Winchester, is now in Steeple Church.

Before the organ was installed the singing was accompanied by a harmonium of an antiquated pattern which, in its younger days, had been devotedly cared for by a former rector's daughter, Eleanor Truell. She kept her treasure at the rectory and let it face the dampness of the church on Sundays only. A trolley was constructed for it and the brawnier members of the congregation loaded it up on Sunday mornings, dragged it to the church, and brought it home again at night.

My father could remember the old barrel organ used at Tyneham in still earlier days. The clerk gave out the metrical psalm appointed to be sung, with the formula :—"Let us sing to the praise and glory of God the hundredth psalm, to "Wareham", or whatever the tune might be, in stentorian monotone. The organ player then began to turn the crank and the tune was creakingly ground out.

When hymns began to supplement the metrical psalms some words or lines had frequently to be repeated in order to fit the tunes. A Sister of the Community of the Epiphany at Truro, now in her nineties, remembers being allowed as a treat to change the tunes in the Steeple barrel-organ when staying at Grange as a child.

I can remember my cousin Eleanor Truell as she was long after her parents' death, when she was living in a little house at Wimborne. Even then she gave an impression of energy and capability. The older Tyneham people could recall how efficiently she ran the rectory household, taught in the school and coped with parish affairs.

Unable to do any entertaining at the rectory on account of her parents' health she devised another means of returning hospitality and asked her friends and neighbours to a mammoth picnic once a year at Worbarrow. My mother has described these gatherings of up to a hundred guests and told us of the elaborate arrangements made by Eleanor for the accommodation of their men and horses. Stabling was booked at all the neighbouring farms and clear instructions posted well beforehand for the information of the coachmen. I believe the feast was spread on the green beyond the coastguard station.

The altar in Tyneham church was solid and heavy, made of oak, a gift from Bishop Hamilton of Salisbury to take the place of some less worthy one in Tractarian times. When I knew it first it had one frontal only, of scarlet cloth embroidered with gold thread in an intricate

all-over pattern. Before I married and went away the church possessed
a set of altar hangings in the Sarum colours. When Martin Travers
designed the memorial to Mrs. Draper he backed the altar with a
lovely shallow reredos* picturing the Crucifixion, under the newly
filled east window .He looked on this east window as among the best
of his achievements. It represents Our Lady seated in the shade of a
weeping willow with the Holy Child upon her knee. The side lights
show, as distant background, miniature scenes of daily life at Tyneham,
fishermen putting out to sea and labourers busy in the fields. The
figures are surrounded by clear glass, allowing the trees and hills to be
seen beyond them. On sunny days the painted butterflies which flutter
round the central group appeared to have floated in, that very moment,
from the outside air, ready to drift away again into the blue. My
mother's Camberwell Beauty is depicted resting with wings outspread
on a fold of Mary's robe. The window, by the kindness of the Church
authorities at Corfe, has found a refuge there.

The ancient altar vessels, worn to paper thinness by their centuries
of use, were of Elizabethan date.

A lancet window on the south side of the sanctuary was filled with
glass by Powell to my design in memory of my husband's father and
has a standing figure of S. Bartholomew, bearing the weapon of his
martyrdom, his eyes turned to the altar. At the base of the window are
the words :—"Remember Nathaniel Bond and glorify God".

Transepts and chancel were all roofed with stone, the nave with
lead, stripped off and stolen since the evacuation.

The ropes from the two bells in an open bell-cote passed in lead
channels through the roof at the top of the chancel arch. I remember
the ringer standing on the step of the chancel facing the people, with a
rope in either hand, a trying position for a bashful lad. The choir were
obliged to duck under the ropes to reach their places. Later the ropes
were reaved through blocks and brought together at one side of the
arch. Above the roof the ropes gave place to chains attached to the bell
cranks and the chains bore metal discs to keep the wet from running
down the channels into the church. The clatter of the discs upon the
tops of the leaden pipes made noise enough to drown the voices of the
bells to those who sat in church. Like many ancient country bells the
Tyneham pair were not attuned or, if they had been once in harmony,
had long since lost their pitch. The voice of one bell had an audible
crack, but their cheerful ting-tang was a lovable sound, like an echo of
the sheep bells on the hills.

I find it difficult to write of what the church meant to its children to
whom it was as dear and as familiar as their homes. I cannot do more

* Now in Steeple Church.

than mention a few random memories of special or of ordinary happenings within its walls.

The sober householders and housewives sat in the nave, the lads and young men in the gallery. The seats in the north transept, rudely called "The Cowstalls" held the rectory family, the clerk, and most of the unattached components of the congregation. It was here that the campers, scouts and summer lodgers squeezed into the pews on summer Sundays when the whole church was packed to suffocation point and not a breath of air was felt to penetrate the open doors and windows. How good it was to hear the Dorset voices letting themselves go in well known psalms and hymns. I can remember so many Easter mornings, with everyone in their very best suits and bonnets, wearing "something new and something blue and something borrowed", and the scents of primrose, daffodil, golden palm and flowering currant filling the air.

And Christmas services—the gallery and pulpit garlanded with glossy evergreens, window sills lined with holly boughs and all the crowded congregation shouting "*In excelsis gloria!*" It was a heartening experience to take part in the ancient carols sung in the vernacular and, though our range was somewhat limited, we thoroughly enjoyed the few we knew. The list included the as yet unhackneyed: "First Nowell", "A Child this day is born", "Good Christian men, rejoice"—to a version of the tune "*In dulce jubilo*"—"Like silver lamps in a distant shrine" and, for Epiphany, "We three Kings of Orient are", all with good swinging airs and simple burdens.

The Harvest Thanksgivings were memorable, too, in the brief pause between the end of one year's labour and the beginning of the next, expressing as they did the gratitude of men who knew the hazards of the seasons and their own dependence for the harvest upon something greater than their labours. I never hear the lively strains announcing that :—

"The valleys stand so thick with corn
That even they are singing",

or the tramping measure of :—

"We plough the fields and scatter
The good seed o'er the land",

without recalling homely, earthy smells of corn and apples, dahlias, China asters, Sunday clothes, oil lamps and new-baked bread.

We once at least adorned the gallery with clean new lobster pots, intending to complete the decoration with a seine, but the fishing nets were all too reminiscent of the summer's catches and we had to make do with the rector's tennis net.

On the first Sunday following a funeral the family of the deceased appeared in force and in unrelieved black garments, sitting throughout the service and merely leaning forward, with gloved hands shading faces, during prayers. By custom it was incorrect for the bereaved to stand or kneel at their first attendance after the interment.

We had a close-up view of baptisms, the font being just outside the south transept screen, and took keen personal interest in the christening of our future Sunday scholars. Sometimes the parents asked us for suggestions for the baby's name, especially when the family was a long one and kinsfolk's names had all been used for older brethren.

Occasionally, uninvited worshippers appeared in church and there were painful efforts to look unconcerned when bats swooped up and down the nave and in and out of transepts, causing the female members of the congregation to bend before their coming like a field of corn before the wind.

Cats sometimes followed outraged owners into church and once my own was the offender, swaggering up the nave with vertical tail and into the pulpit, to my deepfelt shame.

Many years afterwards my brother's wife was the sole occupant of the south transept on a drowsy Sunday afternoon. She heard, as she fancied, some late comer steal to the open door and, after a moment's silence, scuffling and bumping in the seats at the back without any visible cause. Her curiosity was roused and she got up to investigate, finding two well grown lambs engaged in a butting contest under a pew.

The churchyard was immaculately kept while Mr. Homan was incumbent. He levelled ground between the graves and bordering the paths, keeping it shaved with his own mowing machine. The rest of the grass was cut with scythe and hook.

Snowdrops, crocuses, primroses and cyclamen had spread from graves and made themselves at home in every corner.

The graves of unknown seafarers, cast up by the sea from time to time, lay sheltered under the chancel wall.

A little avenue of elm trees lined the path across the churchyard by the rectory garden wall. Most of these trees were very old and had been pollarded for safety's sake but had grown some good-sized tops again.

CHAPTER XI

Comings and Goings

WHEN I look back upon how we entertained ourselves before the first world war it strikes me as unlikely that a younger generation can possibly believe in happiness obtained so simply. Yet to our unsophisticated minds such pastoral pleasures as a choir or school treat did give unalloyed enjoyment.

Choir treats were winter fixtures at the rectory and, after sumptuous teas, the dining-room was cleared for round games and dumb crambo.

The favourite rendezvous for summer school treats was the shore at Worbarrow. Steeple and Grange contingents came in waggons decked with evergreens and flags, the excited children singing loud enough to drown the chiming of the horse-bells.

After a mammoth tea we raced for prizes, went for trips in boats, or played traditional games on the green by the coastguard station; "I sent a letter to my love", "Tom Tiddler's ground" and "Flags", "The farmer in the dell" (whose tiresomely monotonous domestic history, recited to a perfectly maddening time, only wore to an end in order to begin all over again), "Twos and Threes", "Oranges and Lemons", "Nuts in May" and the ancient "We are the Roman soldiers", till paws became too sticky to be held and everyone collapsed exhausted on the grass. Then the big jugs of lemonade went round, with buns and oranges, before the waggons loaded up again and rolled away into the dusk. The children's cheering sounded, ever fainter, long after they and the waggons had been lost to sight.

The school treats were the great occasions of our youthful summers and, like other parish frolics, were enjoyed by all alike. We took our entertainments where we found them, from sources common to us all, and shared the pleasure and amusement they provided.

The common interests of a small and self-contained community bound us together in a close relationship such as can seldom be the case in less remote surroundings. Where all were bred on the land, stemming from forebears who had never left it, the love of the land was in the blood and its welfare paramount. Its processes were the close concern of each and all, and everybody shared the same anxieties and satisfactions with regard to them. The lives of us all were rooted in the soil and the simple, basic interests of men's life in country places were the common topics of our talk, making for perfect sympathy and understanding.

If long connection with the land produced stability and strength of character, the sharing of it did away with class obsession. No feeling of the sort created obstacles to unselfconscious friendship. It was not until my lot was cast in a town that I found myself confronted by the odious tyranny of class distinctions and the least pleasant types of snobbery, both ordinary and inverted. The many social grades and watertight compartments of town life surprised and saddened me.

At Tyneham everyone pursued his own vocation in his special walk of life without encroaching on his neighbour's, but snobbery was happily unknown.

Besides the choir and school treats there were Christmas parties in the school or brewhouse and parish outings in the summer.

Our entertainments from without came in the form of travellers, a colourful string of whom appeared at regular intervals throughout the year. Among these were the knife-grinder, old Stanley, a well-known figure in the southern counties, with "Lovey" his ancient wife, both weathered to the colour of mahogany from constant tramping of the roads.

There were Italian organ-grinders accompanied by dreadfully human monkeys in little red coats or by a pair of love-birds, taught to pick out "fortunes" printed on gay paper slips and pass them to the shy enquirer in exchange for a penny.

Sometimes a gipsy came, in a bright head handkerchief, with odds and ends of ribbons and laces to sell, and the kindly colporteur would visit us, doing brisk trade at the kitchen door with books from the pack strapped to his shoulders.

Poor dusty, footsore bears were still allowed to travel the country roads with their Greek or Pyrenean masters. The only pleasure these poor creatures gave us was that of seeing them plunge their heads and paws into the pails of water that we hastened to put before them.

Once, I recall, a frayed old couple "from the Lyceum Theatre, London", for some inexplicable reason made their way to Tyneham where they staged an impromptu entertainment in the school before a hurriedly gathered and bewildered audience.

Best loved of all our visitants was a sad and gentle hurdy-gurdy man, surely the last of all his race, whose hushed and melancholy rendering of "The Farmer's Boy" was hauntingly re-echoed from the Old House walls, like a snatch of music from a long-dead past.

I can remember, too, the sudden burst of sound from voices singing in the night, when the Church Knowle choirmen made their carol-singing round at Christmas time.

Our family recreations oftenest took the form of walks together more especially in winter. These sometimes took us to the end of Flower's Barrow, to look down upon the Lulworth woods and pastures fringing the dark expanse of heath land to the north. On days when wreaths of fog lay out in the Channel, ready to roll inland and hide the valley at our feet, the tale of the Phantom Army came to mind, the story of the armed battalions which, on the evidence of many witnesses, marched from the Roman 'rings' along the hill in 1678. "A vast number of soldiers, several thousands", says Hutchins' *History of Dorset,* "were seen marching towards Grange one December evening, with a great noise and clashing of arms". They are said to have been seen by Captain John Lawrence, who then lived at Grange, by his brother and about one hundred more, "particularly by four clay-cutters just going to leave off work and by all the people in the cottages and hamlets thereabout, who left their supper and houses and came to Wareham and alarmed the town" . . . "Three hundred of the militia were marched to Wareham . . . Captain Lawrence and his brother went post to London and deposed the particulars on oath before the Council, and had not his family been of known affection to the government he would have been severely punished, the nation being in a ferment about Oates' plot".

Some of my earliest memories are of picnics down at Broadbench, afternoons of sheer delight. When cousins from Grange were occupying Egliston we knew that we should find a kind and affectionate welcome at the little house. My first remembrance in connection with a Broadbench picnic is of being driven there in the two-wheeled luggage-cart by Sydney Mills. I can still hear the ring and slither of the iron shoes and tyres on the then unbroken stones of Shoemakers Lane and see the sunlight flickering through the deep green shade to dapple the horse's coat. The cart, proceeding at a foot's pace, rocked and bumped across the Upper Horse Close, with a pleasing sideways tilt which made me cling to Sidney's sleeve. Then came the thrilling descent of the other side of the hill. After the first and steepest pitch we steered a zigzag course to ease the drop as far as possible. But even so it must have been anxious business for the driver, and I often wonder now how the great horse kept on his feet on the breakneck track. About halfway down, the so-called road petered out in grass as slippery as itself. So, with much lurching over emmet butts and into rabbit holes we came in triumph to the top of the cliff, where we left the cart and scrambled down the stairway, cut in the shale by my father-in-law-to-be, to the shelf of rock below. Broadbench's level platform stretched away round the foot of the cliff to the west into Hobarrow Bay. At its seaward edge it formed a small cliff of its own where the upper shelf ended a few feet above a boulder strewn floor. This miniature cliff was indented and had little headlands and inlets where rock pools held bright sea anemones. The shelf made an excellent table for picnics and legs could be comfortably swung as the picnicker sat on the edge overlooking the four foot abyss. At low tide the games to be played round the rocks and ankle-deep basins of clear, lukewarm water were legion. I can still feel the warmth of the smooth, sleek rock face on the soles of my feet.

Near the foot of the cliff there were shells to be found but they could not compare with the treasures abounding along the high water mark in the next cove to the east, known as Sharnal, to be reached by an arduous climb over rocks.

The shells lay in myriads on the fine shale of the shore, among them small cowries much cherished by us as counters for games. There, too, was a large choice of wentletraps, razor-shells, limpets and whelks. But the charm of the inexhaustible store lay in thousands of infinitesimal shells too small to be noticed at all except at very close range. Each one was a miracle of perfection. There were fairylike spirals of spindle-shells, almost invisible needle-whelks, lovely, diminutive top shells in infinite modifications of colour, rose-pink and purple and lavender, pencilled in shades of warm brown, red and wine. There were frail little limpet-shaped shells, transparent and golden and dotted with hair-slender, turquoise-blue lines. There were shells that we called "pheasant shells", patterned over with feather-like markings, and miniature winkles, red, orange and brown, chocolate, yellow and grey.

The pools were a garden of sea weeds, where sprays of the finer varieties were plucked to be taken home and floated out on cards, their delicate fronds being patiently spread and arranged with the point of a pin.

At the end of the day we went back up the Egliston Gwyle, at first through high copse wood that arched overhead to form a green tunnel. Near the top of the wood the pathway came out in a clear, open glade and beyond it appeared the charming low Georgian cottage with its row of French windows and long paved verandah. The small semicircular grass plot in front of the house was ringed with bright flowering shrubs, hydrangeas and fuchsias, montbretia and myrtle, and sheltered by ilexes, sycamores, chestnuts and yews. A peephole cut out in the trees framed a view of the sea.

If Tyneham was quiet and remote, South Egliston was yet more isolated, unget-at-able except by rough grass tracks from Kimmeridge and the Tyneham valley. My twice great-grandfather, John of Tyneham and Grange, purchased the property in 1760, giving it to his second son, the Reverend Denis, at that time the incumbent of Steeple-cum-Tyneham, who built the house and spent the greater portion of his life in it until his death at the age of 87. Great-uncle Nat of Grange, when he succeeded to South Egliston, built on additons to the house and my husband's parents used it as a holiday cottage for their family. My mother-in-law had a particular affection for the place and loved to spend long periods of the summer there with relays of her eleven sons and daughters. Old Gover cared for the Gwyle and garden during many years, tramping the long road with its double hill climb from his cottage at East Creech. Nor did he lie abed or put his feet up on a Sunday as he might have done, but acted organist to Grange and Steeple churches and never missed a service. He was a typical represent-

ative of a hardy Dorset stock with a lively sense of duty, and it is note-
worthy that his own generation took him very much for granted.

South Egliston was neighboured closely by the two South Tyneham houses, one of them occupied as a holiday home by Mr. Drew, the
Wareham ironmonger, the other by the cattleman in charge of the
young stock grazing on South Tyneham.

It must have been a lonely spot for him and his in winter when the
other cottages were empty and the south-west gales came roaring in,
unchecked by any wind-break, from the near-by Channel, but the
family who lived there seemed contented with their home and the wife
had plenty of pluck and spirit. She regularly walked to Wareham for
her shopping, crossing two formidable hills, undaunted by the wet
unmetalled tracks from Egliston to Steeple Leaze. Once on the summit
of the second hill, where the road dropped down to Grange, she would
change her heavy boots and muddied petticoats for town attire at the
edge of the wood. The boots and clothing, pushed beneath a sheltering
hazel mock, were a familiar sight to passersby. My sister often picked
their owner and her parcels up on her homeward way from Wareham
but Mrs. X made nothing of the fourteen miles of hilly walking.

When we grew older and could go to Egliston on foot we found
the climb back over the hill a strain on tired muscles. The footpath up
through Parson's Mead, disdaining circuits, always seemed to be the
longest, steepest scramble in the parish.

Picnics at Arishmel were not so popular with us as those at Broadbench, involving as they did a voyage in the dinghy and less to interest
children at the end of it.

While Colonel Blake and his family lived at Smedmore at the turn
of the century the grass on the hill track between Kimmeridge and
Tyneham had little time to grow. We ran the three miles there and
back in summer "after teas" and on Saturday half holidays, unless it
was the Smedmore children's turn to come to Tyneham. We eight
girls, much of an age, spent hours together playing cricket, hockey or
other games, according to the season, and in paper chases which in
time became a weekly institution, taking us for long runs across the
country. One of the farmers on whose land we "hunted" said that so
far as he was concerned we might go wherever we liked about his farm,
because he could trust us not to frighten cattle, break a fence, trespass
on crops or leave a gate unfastened, a tribute which at that time ranked
with us as the highest possible compliment.

If only townsfolk would conform to the few and simple rules of
country courtesy how welcome they would be in rural areas.

CHAPTER XII

Times and Seasons

MY father used to speak of winters in his youth when the outdoor men accompanied the carriage to the top of the Knap, holding it down by means of ropes passed over the roof, as his aunts set out on a journey in a gale.

Snow did not often visit Tyneham but when it did it caused considerable inconveniences. The hill roads soon became impassable and sometimes the valley road as well. If it lasted more than a few days the men would struggle into Wareham carrying sacks and come back loaded up with bread and meat. The heaviest falls came in from the south-east.

On one occasion, about 1899, the snow on the lawn was deep enough to provide material for a large snow elephant.

Another fall that I remember came on a 26th of April. Exactly one week later, at the Bath and West of England Show at Dorchester, people were fainting from the heat of the sun.

The Purbeck valley was practically free from autumn and winter mists. At other times the Channel fogs were never far away and liable to come rolling in so swiftly that the Tyneham dwellers learned to be prepared for them at any moment.

It might be a grilling summer's day with a cloudless sky, when suddenly the scene would disappear behind a drifting curtain of white vapour, with a chilling drop of temperature. We never thought of wearing thin summer frocks except for going "inland". No fall of the barometer gave warning of the coming change. The glass had probably stood high for days, with all the other weather portents favourable, so that the prospects for a fête or outing seemed most promising. Then all at once a cold air crept up from the sea, followed immediately by clinging, blinding fog and the mournful lowing of the Shambles lightship, voicing its hoarse monotonous complaint. These sea mists had the advantage of keeping the valley green and, even in the longest of dry spells, the pastures held good grazing, while lawns and garden remained fresh and bright.

The fogs could be alarming to a stranger unfamiliar with the lie of the land.

The fishermen could reckon their position when befogged at sea by the sound of the surf on different parts of the shore and the echo from the faces of the several cliffs, although to us the hollow and eerie reverberations of the seagulls' cries or the noise of the oars, tossed back from the unseen walls of rock, seemed all alike.

There were days when the fog was dense enough to limit the range of vision to a yard or so. At such times it was well to know and recognize each tree and bush, each gate and angle of a wall.

Often a salty gale would brown and shrivel leaves in early summer and Tyneham lacked the gorgeous autumn colouring to be seen inland. But there was colour enough for those who had an eye for it and, even in unfavourable seasons, plenty of satisfying patches in the sheltered places; flat, jonquil-yellow washes where the elms predominated and here and there a birch's bright gold coinage strung on slender sprays. In the terrace garden beeches trailed their flattened tiers of tawny leaves, like the sweep of a peacock's tail, and coppice and hedgerow held their brilliant foliage even when rain and wind had stripped the tall trees bare. Field maples flamed along the fences, with scarlet spindle, greenish gold of hazel, whitethorn's dusky reds and the incongruous note of elder bushes, madder, rose and ashy pink.

What struck the stranger most on coming first to Tyneham in the dead of the year was the warmth of winter colouring. The valley never lost its glow, and though its colours were subdued, they shone on sunlit days with the soft refulgence of a Sandby water-colour drawing. The colder greys of hills and woods up-country here gave place to every kind of brown, from the pale buff of the rowaty grass, like an old lion's mane, through all the range of bistre, mushroom, russet, cocoa, raisin, rust and cinnamon shades of hedge and coppice to the deep brown-madder of the plough grounds.

In the heart of the woods the leaves hung tawny all the winter through on the lichen-whitened oaks. The seedling oaks' leaves were of a deeper tan and dangled from the twigs like little dogskin gloves. The birch brush looked, from a distance, like a cloud of lilac smoke deepening to plum and wine-red colours as the spring drew on, and the dog-wood stems glowed crimson.

The open winters kept the fields and meadows green—soft pastel greens, opaque and flat except when seen against the sunlight, when they shone translucent as clear water.

A Purbeck characteristic was the frequency of withy-beds, the small enclosures set with willow stocks providing osiers for the lobster pots. Round Tyneham there were half a dozen or more, a patch in Way-ground and another occupying part of Rook Grove, a larger bed at Baltington and plantings at the sea end of the Gwyle, as well as in the dairyman's and Alfred Tizzard's gardens. Besides these there were sallows in the herb garden at the House, for all the garden baskets were home-made by the gardeners in weather which made outdoor work impossible. These withies added yet another brilliant note of colour to the winter scene, reflected by the Indian reds of bracken on the hill.

For those who have a dread of thunderstorms the neighbourhood of Purbeck can be recommended as a refuge. The storms that visit it are few and far between and seldom very violent.

The Tyneham rainfall was considerably lower than the amount recorded on the north side of the hill, and there were rarely extremes of cold or heat.

The local weather lore was based on centuries of observation and was a good deal more reliable for the particular locality than were the official forecasts.

To hear the sea on Broadbench "roaring" was to be sure that a storm was brewing up, and the smell of Kimmeridge seaweed foretold rain. If ring doves sang before Christmas then the winter would be mild.

A thrush heard singing "out of season" prophesied approaching rain and, when they heard it, folk would shake their heads at "thic there 'wet-wet' bird".

Oil beetles appearing in the spring were a sign of better days ahead. Rooks tumbling suddenly downwards in their flight foretold rough weather.

A spate of wasps and hazel nuts and babies always came together, according to George Richards. A circle round the moon portended gales :—

"The larger the wheäl
The nearer the geäle."

A special charm of life at Tyneham was its great variety. The country scene was never two days alike and change of seasonal occupation kept in step with the ever changing aspect of the woods and fields.

None with a love of natural things and interested in the rhythm of the country could possibly be dull in such surroundings.

A host of memories of these pleasant, ordinary happenings come crowding to my mind when I look back on those long vanished days.

Outside the House the never ending business of estate and farm went on, so smoothly organised and balanced that each worker fitted into place and had enough but not too much to do the whole year round.

The use of casual labourers was rare and limited to extra help for singling roots. Threshing and sheep-shearing were performed by travelling companies of experts, and Albert Taylor, from Rookery in the heath, dealt ably with the laying of field drainage.

The round of farm routine was livened by the little extra events, the first time that the carthorses went out to grass in spring, when their delighted gambolings and elephantine capers shook the ground and made us share their keen enjoyment of the sudden freedom (if there is any better smell than that of a well-kept horse in a summer meadow, I should like to meet it), the sheep-dipping and, afterwards, the shearing in the barn, the threshing times, the regular grass burnings along the hills and, now and again, the arrival of some newly purchased stock or the excitement when the Devon cattle went off to the county shows. Close to the farmyard, in the Cowleaze, was a four-foot bank, the remnant of some old enclosure. My father had deep grooves cut into the bank to take the rear-wheels of a waggon, so that the beasts could walk along the higher ground and enter the waggon on the level without the fuss of being pushed and dragged up a slippery ramp. All the young beasts were taught to lead in halters from their earliest youth, which simplified their transfer when they left the farm and saved much trouble on the road.

With the end of summer came the blackberrying expeditions and gathering of "snags" to make into sloe gin.

We never gathered blackberries after Michaelmas Day, when they were spat upon by the devil. Good Friday was the proper day for setting potatoes, an old belief connected with the waxing Paschal Moon ? Apart from these I cannot remember many superstitions. It is true that an alarming large black dog was said to haunt the neighbourhood of Boatswain's Coppice on the Lulworth road and that it was reputed to have barred the way to certain persons passing that way late at night, but the legend may have been invented by the village wives to hasten husbands home from the "Weld Arms" betimes.

It was not many miles away from Tyneham that an aunt of mine overheard a conversation in which one of the speakers obstinately held that the nightingale was not a bird at all but a "spirit voice", and that nobody alive had ever seen the singer.

We used to say that if a wasp were killed, another would attend the funeral, but I fancy that this saying is not confined to Dorset.

The cuckoo always came in time for Wareham Fair to buy himself a pair of breeches, whether or no he chose to announce himself that day. Elders were planted outside dairy and larder windows not for superstitious reasons but to keep off flies.

Christmas was still a festival of Church and home, unspoilt by artificially contrived excitements and completely uncommercialised, a time of family gatherings, jollity and good cheer, looked forward to throughout the year. The gifts exchanged on Christmas Day were modest ones compared with the expensive presents which have taken their place.

Our Christmas shopping in person was confined to one day's expedition "down to Bourne", with a visit to Beale's Bazaar, where we tried to find as many presents for the family and household as the little time at our disposal would allow. In those days shopkeepers in town assisted country customers by sending errand boys with parcels to the railway stations. I remember rows of lads on Bournemouth Central platform, calling the names of passengers, who claimed their packages and tipped the messengers before they boarded the train. Apart from this one day we shopped by post, choosing our gifts from the many illustrated catalogues sent out by shops and stores.

Our Christmas cards we bought from Messrs Hill and Churchill's Swanage shop. A cardboard dress-box full of samples came by post and we spent happy evenings choosing from the great variety of cards at prices suited to our slender purses. They were a good deal less artistic in design and finish than the greetings cards on sale to-day, but they seldom cost us more than a penny apiece—some could be had at twenty-four for a shilling—and at least their words and subjects were connected with the Feast.

Mention of prices rouses memories of gold and silver coinage and the astonishing extent of purchasing power.

One of my wedding presents was a book which taught the middle-class housewife how to feed a family really well on a pound a week. The seven dinners cost just 5/6d. and a table gave a detailed menu for each day of the month, varied according to the time of year. The food suggested was both choice and excellent as well as ample. Our grocer's bill was small, with butter at 1/- the pound, tea at 2/-, eggs at a dozen or eighteen to the shilling and other prices in proportion.

My mother's dairy accounts for 1905 record the price of pigmeat sold to Tyneham households. One entry runs as follows :—

		s.	d.
9¼ lb. Loin of pork	. . . . .	5	5
3 lb. Neck of pork	. . . . .	1	6
8¾ lb. Ham	. . . . . .	4	4½
13 lb. Bacon	. . . . . .	5	5
3¼ lb. Spring	. . . . . .	1	4
½ Head	. . . . . .	1	0

Even occasional luxuries and treats were possible to all but the lowest wage earners, with half a dozen bottles of beer for 1/3d. and "Players" at 2½d. for 10. Whisky was 3/6d. the bottle.

Clothing the family, too, though difficult on then current incomes, could somehow be contrived when boys' tweed suits could be had for twelve and fourteen shillings, overcoats for five, hats for one and six-pence and boots from five shillings upwards. A warm serge frock for a little girl might cost not more than half-a-crown and women's clothes were priced to match.

I see from my early dress accounts that woollen stockings cost me one and sixpence; blouses, of better quality than anything that can be purchased now, could be had for a very few shillings from the well-known West End shops, which willingly sent selections down by post "on approval".

One excellent flannel suit I had from Peter Robinson at one and a half guineas, and all but the ultra-expensive shops sold coats and skirts, well-cut and of good materials, at two or three guineas. Seven and six to nine and six was an ordinary price for house shoes, fifteen for stout walking shoes in calf.

Long white kid gloves for dances cost me four-and-six and the charge for cleaning was three halfpence a pair. Tan leather gauntlets cost no more than half-a-crown, short beaver gloves two shillings and suede ones three-and-six a pair.

Harrods provided me with a smart *en-tout-cas* for five shillings; a pair of bedroom slippers for three shillings and satin dancing shoes for four-and-eleven-pence.

And all these things were high in quality, well made and finished and expected to last.

The children had good value for their pennies, too. As Mr. McQueen Pope has said :—"Five shillings would stock a nursery". Yes, and stock it handsomely.

Does anyone besides myself remember the small circular metal musical-boxes, adorned with shiny pictures, which tinkled out sweet, brittle music at the turn of a handle? They cost from sixpence to a shilling and mine, which played untiringly though sometimes jerkily "The Bluebells of Scotland", was an abiding joy.

There were penny dolls, and little lead soldiers several to the penny. Such toys were made to last, as were the rather more expensive models at a shilling or two. Of such was my cherished red tin pump, which pumped real water from a tiny reservoir into an inch-high bucket smelling divinely of its crimson paint, and my Russian egg, a beautiful piece of workmanship, each gaily coloured wooden shell containing another just a trifle smaller exactly fitting into it, until the last one, no bigger than a blackbird's, opened to disclose a solid egg the size of a pea.

The quiet of the valley helped to make of it a sanctuary for all wild life and I have already mentioned some of the flowers and creatures which made their home in it.

Thanks to protection for the birds, both large and small, the "balance of nature" remained undisturbed and there were never any plagues of Egypt. The rabbit population flourished as is its wont and, though little was done to keep it within bounds, it never increased to any burdensome degree. The foxes, badgers, stoats and weasels, ravens, peregrines and buzzards saw to that.

Tyneham was equally free from rodent and insect pests. Red squirrels were common and protected in the earlier years but afterwards became a rarity and finally disappeared. So far as I know, the sinister grey tree rats never found their way to Tyneham.

Roedeer, in ones and twos, occasionally visited the woods and sometimes stayed on for a season. I am told that they are seen there in far greater numbers now.

The South Hill was a favourite haunt of hares. There were several pairs of badgers, seldom appearing in the daytime but making their presence known by terrifying screams on moonlight nights in spring.

The dormouse and the nightingale both passed us by, to our deep regret.

I hear that the smaller birds have left the valley now that it is no longer occupied by man.

Before it was forsaken Tyneham was a paradise for birds and every coppice and hedgerow was "a-charm" with them.

Their voices form a background to my memories and special places are connected always in my mind with special songs of birds.

The long-drawn downward curve of a starling's derisive whistle calls up pictures of the dog-yard on a bright spring morning, the cry of golden plover takes me back to Gold Down under a dark wintry sky, the cushioned voice of a ring dove speaks of scented summer afternoons among the Avenue lines, and May at Tyneham is brought back to me with joy and pain when I hear the rapturous thrilling of the skylarks over high hill pastures.

The garden as I knew it then was musical with thrushes singing their often repeated staves at all times of the year, a blackbird's whistling speaks to me of Rook Grove, thick with primroses and the scream of swifts of the long after-glows of June.

The calls of woodpeckers and jays belong to Avenue and Wood and the metallic notes of titmice to the orchard trees.

The thought of Tyneham cannot be dissociated from the sounds of gulls in infinite variety, from plaintive mewings to the noisy chorus of the pack. The outcry would begin with a single voice, another would join in, then more and more at an increasing tempo until the air was ringing with the clangour, which ceased as quickly as it had begun.

A frog at Tyneham was a nine-days wonder, though toads were in abundance. The village pond was thick with their chains of jelly-like eggs each year.

Hornets were very rare and I cannot remember more than one occasion when a nest of them was found.

The larger dragonflies were fairly common and elegant demoiselles occasionally visited the ponds. The children called them "Horse tingers" and were afraid to touch them, believing that they had a dangerous sting.

Each man employed on the estate was lent a strip of ground (I cannot now remember its extent) for his potato crop. The ground was ploughed and, I think, planted for him. These strips were often in the Lime Kilns and, in certain seasons, quantities of pupae of the death's head moth were found there when the crop was lifted. "Harvesters" were an annual affliction, causing much suffering even to the natives and their dogs as well as to rabbits. Strangers to Purbeck often became feverish and ill from the "bites" of harvesters, which we frustrated to a certain extent by daubing our ankles with carbolic soap.

Because of its remoteness and a long tradition of protective policy, the parish was a preserve for flowers as it was for birds and beasts.

The wildest botanists will fail to drag from me the secrets of the rarer species' hiding-places or even their names.

The commoner plants had local names and local sayings were attached to them.

The greater plantain was a "blackamoor" and furnished weapons for a summer version of the game of "conkers". Wild clematis or traveller's joy was given the uneuphonious but descriptive name of "man's wig", and the house-leek, growing on the mossy tiles of every cottage pigstye, was called "silgreen". It was much prized as a herbal remedy and was still in use, to my knowledge, up to a very short time ago.

Bluebells were "granfer greygles" and mallows "bread and cheese". Tyneham called king-cups or marsh marigolds "may-blobs", and purple orchis "soldiers" or, sometimes, 'giddy ganders". Laburnums bore the lovely nickname "goolden chains" and primroses were always "p'imroses". The creeping buttercup was known as "ram's cla's", and the children made up cowslips into "tissty-tossty" balls. The thought of them evokes their scents and all those other fragrances that cling about the memory of a vanished Tyneham; the summer breath of lime flowers and the earlier incense of the hawthorn blossom; dry-sweet smell of stubbles; cool essences of ferns in watery hollows; the bitter sweet of the fallen sycamore leaves; the slender thread of fragrance from wild strawberry plants; the saddening, aromatic scent of meadow-sweet and the indescribable "smell of woodland wine", all borne on currents of a sea-washed air.

The winds forbade the growth of forest trees except in favoured spots, though patient planting through the years had by degrees formed wind-breaks in whose shelter choicer kinds could grow and prosper. I have no record of the making of the West Plantation but, judging by the age of its silver firs, it must have stood for at least two hundred years. The silvers in the Little Wood at Grange were planted by my great-great-grandfather about the middle of the eighteenth century and may have been contemporaries. They and their cousins at Tyneham reached the limit of their ages and began to fall some years ago.

My father loved all trees, a love inherited and shared by countless country landowners whose forebears changed and beautified the face of England. It may not be too much to claim that, but for the untiring efforts of such men, the country would be treeless save for the scanty remnants of the ancient forests and the surroundings of a few enlightened townships such as Dorchester. The traveller going about the freshly ravaged counties in this year of grace can scarcely fail to notice that the still existing, ever dwindling traces of past sylvan beauty are almost always to be found in the noble groups or stands of trees about some country house.

We learned as youngsters that to plant was an act of faith and public spirit since the planter could expect no personal reward. Each generation felled according to its needs but recognized the duty of replacing what was felled. To cash in on the timber planted by one's forefathers without replanting for the sake of those to come was looked upon as robbery. To this long vision it was due that timber was forthcoming when the need was greatest in the time of war.

It is sad that the love of trees has so declined and that the average Englishman nowadays prefers some oriental midget to his own magnificent native timber. It seems that, in a very few more years, the only specimen trees left in the country will be foreigners, the only woodland vast State Forests of Teutonic trees, where no bird sings or even cares to fly, no wild flowers grow and where a forest fire is a perpetual menace.

To my father every tree was an individual with its individual idiosyncracies which must be studied and indulged to obtain perfection. Felling or lopping was not done except at proper seasons. The present habit of town and country "bodies" (as well as of some private landowners who might be expected to know better) of throwing or hacking timber while the sap is flowing would have roused my father's indignation. How often I have heard him say that elms should never be touched by saw or axe except on the last and first days of the year, a way of printing on our minds the shortness of the season during which the elm is fit to be felled.

He had a deep affection for the elm, as one of the hardiest and finest of our indigenous trees, and he planted many of the different species, favouring Cornish as the type best suited to the Tyneham soil and climate.

When boughs were lopped he trimmed each stump himself with loving care and the wounds healed evenly and quickly, leaving no ugly scar to rot in course of time. He took great pains when planting to secure the perfect place, not only that most favourable to the tree itself but also the position which would show it to the best advantage when it was full grown. For days before he finally decided on the spot in the West Plantation to be filled by a copper beech he marked alternative sites with white-flagged poles and studied them from various points across the valley.

CHAPTER XIII

Odds and Ends

THE rich and racy Dorset dialect is vanishing so fast before the language of the B.B.C., genteel and colourless, that it may be worth recording a few words in daily use at Tyneham not so very long ago, some of them not included in the glossary to William Barnes' "Poems of Rural Life". The faggots carried home by hedgers at the end of the day were known as *nitches*, the smaller ones of kindling wood as *nickies*. *Writh* in the Purbeck parlance meant all small, light brushwood, not only the small wreath of wands employed in hurdling, as the glossary defines it. The stumps of ash and hazel whence the new growth sprang up after copsing were *mocks* and a roughly constructed cage for catching pheasants a *nicklyvat*.

Snakes were politely known as *eëls* and sloes were *snags*.

To throw a stone or stick at an animal or other target was to *squail* it. 'Elevenses' was *nammut*.

The sea, when showing phosphorescent light at night, was said to be *bremming*.

A pole or clothes prop was a *promp* ; a strut, as used in fencing, was a *scote* and part of a fishing line a *snood*.

Jam jars were always *gallipots*.

Sumpling, a useful word, I think, meant softening or limbering up, *tackling* was walking with a plodding or rolling gait, *e.g.*: "I seed 'un tacklen up drough groun', *ground* being the word employed for arable land.

A horse or person *lumpered* instead of stumbling, and ground churned up or poached by the feet of cattle was "all of a *puxie*", while stones that were rough and nobbly were described as *numbly*. A culvert or short length of drain was known as a *bunny*, where rabbits might *crope* but never 'creep'. One *hurdled* or *hardled* the poor rabbits, after death, by slitting one hind leg and passing the other one through it to make hanging easier.

Whur frost was Purbeck for hoar frost.

Scarecrows were *mommuts*, objects *plimmed* instead of swelling, if one felt queer or shaky one was *leary*. To *croop* or *croopy* was to crouch.

The fishermen would talk of the weather being *caffety* in the sense of being uncertain or unsettled, and Henry Miller used the expressive synonym of *cloggy* for being drunk.

Lounging, at Tyneham, became *lunging*, notches, *snotches*. When jostled or bewildered by a crowd one was *scrushed* and *bumbled*.

Charm was a term employed to describe a shivering or vibrating sound like the loud chiming of a peal of bells or the twittering of birds.

I believe that the expression *rowaty* for rough, coarse grass is derived from the *Norman* dialect.

Pebbles we knew as *popples*.

Drongways or *drongs* were narrow closed-in lanes or passages.

An *oont* or *wont* was a mole, *emmuts* were ants and an *emmut butt* an anthill. A newt was an *evet*.

We *panked*, a better word, than 'panted' to my mind, and when we flattened things or knocked them down we *squotted* them.

A beetle (tool) was a *biddle* and a winch a *wink*.

A soft and simple person was called a *sammy*; a gap in a fence or wall a *shard*, and a smother of smoke or dust, a *smeech*.

The frameworks fitted to the waggon-tops for loads of hay or straw were known as *reāves*. In Hampshire they were '*laders*'.

Cows *bleared* instead of lowing, and sought shelter in the *lew*, away from the wind. *Rafty* was wild or enraged when applied to a beast. Apples, potatoes and the like were *pummied* when reduced to pulp.

A ghost and the place where it appeared was called a *hant*.

Instead of rattling, we talked of *rottling*; across became *athirt*.

Caddle was used to describe a muddle, mess or fuss; *nesh* meant soft, tender or delicate; *suant*, supple, soft and workable.

We shared with the rest of the county the good Dorset phrase: "To be shrammed with the cold".

Initial W's had a way of disappearing, as in '*ood*, '*oont* (wont or mole), '*ould*, '*ouldn't*, '*oman*, to reappear in front of '*oak*', '*old*', '*hoar*' transforming them to *woak*, *wold*, *whur*. Husbands referred to "my wold 'oman".

The L was sounded in such words as '*calm*' and '*palm*'.

Th became *D* before a number of words (was this only when followed by R?) such as *dree*, *dreaten*, *dreppence*, *drush*, *dreshing* and *drow*, and an ultimate *Y* was tacked on to some others, *e.g.* *trembly* and *croopy* for 'tremble' and 'crouch'. Yet it dropped from the ends of both 'carry' and 'quarry' (*carr* and *quarr* in our tongue), and from 'yet' and 'not yet', which were changed in to *eet* and *neet*. The plurals of various nouns took additional '*e*'*s*', turning 'posts' into *postes* and 'nests' into *nestes* or *nesses*.

In a good many cases the vowels were altered, as in *brimbles* for 'brambles' and *scritching* for 'screeching', while '*scratching*' became *scrotching*.

The final *T* was suppressed in such negatives as *did'n*, *hadn'*, *couldn'*. The pronoun "it" was very seldom used, except as a 't' in '*tidn*', and was replaced by *er* when in the nominative case, by *en* or *un* in the accusative. In "is not" and in "was not", *S* became a *D*, as *idn'*, *wadn'*, and *wurdn'*, and the harsh-sounding "might not" was softened into "*midden*".

The general effect of the local speech was musical and soft and pleasant to the ear. It is strange that speaking with a Dorset intonation is accounted "common" or uneducated while transatlantic vulgarisms or the mincing accents of "refainement" pass for culture.

The Tyneham icicles were *tinklebobs* or *tinkleybobs* and cuckoos there were *guckoos*.

There was a warm and homely sound about '*my zon*' or '*my zonny*' and I prefer '*my little meaid* or *meäden*' to 'my gurl'.

Narn stood for 'none' and *nary oon* for 'never a one' or 'nobody', as *ary oon* did for 'every one'.

Until quite recently the men still wore the traditional working clothes which stood them in good stead. Smocks had gone out before my time, and old George Richards, well up in his eighties, was their only wearer, though I can remember many of the older men still faithful to them in West Hampshire in the 'nineties. For work in the fields the men had corduroy trousers, strapped sensibly with 'yarks' below the knee, and a strong, thick shirt to shield them from the sun and stinging insects. White linen hats or ancient straws were the universal wear for haymaking and harvesting, with brim enough to shade the eyes and give some cover to the neck. Some of the younger ones had taken to cloth caps worn Geordie fashion, back to front, an innovation which had found no favour with their elders.

All working boots were hobbed and dubbined, giving a maximum of watertightness. So treated they withstood the wettest of conditions, keeping the feet dry even when work had to be done while standing in water.

We children wore goloshes in wet weather, held on by string against the pull of the clay. We once tried heavy wood-soled clogs from Scotland and found them warm and comfortable to wear about the garden but too unyielding for rough, hillside walking. The same firm that supplied them sent us strong brogued shoes of waterproof brown leather at five shillings the pair.

In my father's youth every woman in the country put on pattens to go outside her door in muddy weather. The women of South Petherton walked nine miles into Yeovil on their pattens once a week, taking the gloves which they had finished for the makers and coming back dry-shod with a fresh supply of cut-out skins to stitch.

Familar things in common use at Tyneham up to recent times are disappearing fast, so perhaps it may be of interest to enumerate a few. One was the huge, elliptical, copper vessel, with a handle at each end, to hold hot water for the regular airing of the spare room beds. It made a most efficient warming-pan.

All bedrooms were equipped with nightlights set in shaded burners, in addition to a pair of more of candles. At nightfall bedroom candlesticks, flat silver ones and some of brass with cylinder-shaped glass shades, were set out on a table in the hall.

Now that our eyes have grown accustomed to electric lamps the light of a candle only serves to accentuate the surrounding darkness. We managed, then, to dress and read and mend contentedly by the flickering beams of a couple of "paraffin" candles.

Each room was furnished with a stoneware footbath and a hip bath, set out on a bath rug over night or brought in in the morning.

A tin container shaped somewhat like a shoe and fitted with a lid was used for mulling ale, being thrust into the fire by means of a handle on the "heel".

Foot warmers, long flat tins with a covering of carpet, were filled with boiling water and placed upon the floor of the brougham for winter journeys.

Water for tea-making came to the table in silver or copper urns. A metal rod, made red-hot in the kitchen fire, fitted a cylinder inside the urn and kept the water at boiling point for a considerable time.

Decanters stood in Sheffield coasters on the dinner table, and the beer in the servants' hall was circulated on a fiddle-shaped wooden coaster bound with copper and mounted on little wheels.

I have already spoken of the roasting jack and screen. Another kitchen implement in constant use was the alabaster mortar with its marble-headed pestle. To judge from the number of these costly mortars to be seen on rubbish heaps or forming part of urban rockeries their use in the kitchen must be out of fashion, though nothing equals them in crushing operations.

A roomy wooden flour bin beneath the window was a prominent feature of the Tyneham kitchen. It held sufficient flour to keep the household fed for several weeks.

The oaken press for table-linen is still in my family's possession. The damask cloths and napkins, slightly damped, were placed beneath its massive weight and screw, emerging in knife-edge folds.

Are yokes still used for carrying buckets? The odd man wore one, cunningly shaped in wood to fit his shoulders and take the weight he carried.

All stable buckets were of wood, bound round with iron bands, too heavy for the horses to capsize and free from dangerous sharp edges.

Corn measures were made of birchwood bent to a perfect circle, without any reinforcement and yet strong and enduring.

The shovels for grain were also fashioned from a single piece of wood, exactly fitted to their purpose and very light in hand.

The coachman, when he washed the carriages, wore heavy clogs with leather guards which reached to well above the knee.

A common household object long since vanished, to my great regret, was the box-shaped mouse-trap, easy to set, with nothing to get out of order, harmless to children and domestic animals, merciful to the mouse and practically everlasting. A heavy block of wood fell on the victim and killed it instantaneously.

A specimen of this type of trap is shown in Shakespeare's birthplace and may well have been of use in Tudor times.

Another efficient trap for mice was the 'figure of 4', much favoured by the outdoor men, and the gardeners used it with a fall-trap cleverly contrived with heavy tiles.

Moles were still caught by means of a wire noose set in their runs and attached to a bent withy wand fixed firmly in the ground. When the animal's neck was in the noose the withy sprang upright, and the 'oonts, suspended from their little gallows, were a pathetic and familiar sight of the grass pastures.

We never started for a drive without a stone-pick for the horses' feet, a necessary implement when roads were mended with loose flints indifferently rolled.

The brougham had its 'shoe', a heavy iron skid, hung on a chain beneath its floor, and this was applied to one of the wheels at each descending of Wood Lane. Adjusting the shoe was a tricky affair and taking it off at the foot of the hill was still less agreeable. By that time the iron had grown dangerously hot and awkward to handle. Replacing the shoe on its hook with an arm through the spokes of a well-muddied wheel, while the horses fidgeted and threatened to crush an unskilful hand, was not an enviable task. This and the opening of the gates devolved upon the youngest of the party.

In spite of minor drawbacks such as these the horse-drawn journeys gave us great enjoyment. The fascination of a living and intelligent 'engine', sharing the driver's interest in the way and unpredictable in its reactions, outweighed any disadvantages.

I must confess that the clouds of dust from untarred roads was a plague which I am glad to have outlived. Against it must be set the attraction of the different coloured roads, each characteristic of its district and in harmony with its surroundings.

CHAPTER XIV

Friends and Neighbours

Ave atque vale

BEFORE all men and women were compressed into an anonymous mould we claimed our privileged place as members of a family, a parish and a district. It was our pride to be a Tizzard, Stickland, Miller, Chilcott, Gould or Bond and after that, to form a part of Tyneham, Purbeck and the eastern marches of our county. In spite of friendly rivalries between adjoining villages a common patriotism bound us all, so that we pulled together when the need arose.

An instance of this solidarity occurred in 1900, when my elder brother was brought back, a physical wreck, from the siege of Ladysmith where he had been badly wounded at the assault on Surprise Hill.

The whole neighbourhood joined in welcoming him home, Wareham was flagged and decorated to receive him and the townsfolk, headed by the Mayor, turned out in force to share our happiness, taking the horses from our carriage and dragging it through the streets.

An even heartier welcome awaited my brother at Tyneham. The people gathered under a triumphal arch at the Wayground boundary and again the horses were dispensed with while the men of the parish brought him home.

It was as if our small community were all one family and rejoiced together.

I have already mentioned many Tyneham worthies but find I have said little of the outer ring of neighbours, few and far between but making up for their fewness by their quality.

The first to come to mind are the Purbeck doctors, a tough and gallant race who covered countless miles in the course of the year, by lanes and tracks, through gates and bars, to reach their scattered patients.

The doctor's dog-cart, jogging along the skyline on the ridge of the downs, was a common sight enough, and the trouble he took to visit cases off the beaten track was largely taken for granted.

When answering calls at night the doctors usually forbore to rouse their grooms and put their horses to for themselves. One, practising at Corfe, was of less than medium height and fought nocturnal battles with his horse, which showed its indignation at being roused from sleep by throwing up its head beyond its master's reach. The poor man had to climb into the manger to get the collar and bridle into place. He finally took to riding on his rounds, often a wet and chilly business cheerfully accomplished. A Wareham colleague, known as an eccentric, took a boy on horseback with him to Grange when called to Tyneham and had himself and his bicycle towed at a gallop up Wood Lane. For the most part these good friends in need were loth to press their poorer patients for their fees and often overlooked the fact that they were never paid. They were perforce, at least at Corfe, their own dispensers.

Dr. Godfrey Dru Drury, our family doctor and honoured and loved friend for fifty years, was an outstanding personality in the Purbeck scene. The memory of his sterling character, devoted Churchmanship and unselfish kindness will long remain.

There were unusual characters in the country round about, whose sayings and doings became cherished legends, adding to the spice of life.

A tenant of Smedmore kept a dashing tandem and drove his frightened wife at a reckless speed up and down the Devil's Staircase.

A neighbouring rector, wearing carpet slippers, was wont to drive in a donkey cart to serve a distant church within his cure.

For many years a strange old man whose past was veiled in mystery found hospitality in barns and outhouses. His claim to distinction was his boast of saying the Our Father backwards quicker than any challenger could say it forwards. His charge for the performance was a sixpenny piece.

Our clocks were cared for by our old friend, Mr. Fordham, who came to Tyneham on his bicycle once a week from Wareham at an annual charge of one pound.

As for our pianos, they were tuned for many years by Mr. McIsaac, who travelled by train from Bournemouth, disembarked at Wareham and walked the hilly miles to Tyneham in a frock coat and tall hat.

A Kimmeridge man, Fred Whiterow, mended our shoes, collecting them at regular intervals in a sack slung over his back.

We had a regular and welcome visitor in Mrs. Augustus Foster who "tripped", as she liked to call it, from her cottage at East Lulworth over heath and hill, disdaining roads and taking rough short cuts but looking as neat and well groomed at her journey's end as if she had driven all the way in a carriage and pair. She wore a long, dark petticoat and kilted up her ankle-length black dress well out of the wet. On reaching Tyneham she pulled off her draggled petticoat and sent it by the footman to be dried at the kitchen fire while she had her tea. She kept these expeditions up until she was over seventy.

Before she settled at Lulworth she had lived at Holworth and had regularly "tripped" to early Mass at Lulworth, a good six miles from point to point, by circuitous downland paths.

The friendship between Welds and Bonds withstood the test of centuries and, during penal times, when to possess a horse was, for a

Roman Catholic, a punishable crime, my family's stables housed mysterious animals which were "lent" to Lulworth Castle when required.

As time went on the summer lodgers came as regularly as the swallows. Each year a Sunday dawned when their familiar figures appeared in church again and proved that summer really had arrived.

The pioneers came back again and again. I think one family was faithful to Sea Cottage for some thirty years.

These friends were always welcome and became a valued part of the community.

It was not until much later days that some lapses from good manners and consideration for the native population caused resentment. The valley dwellers somewhat naturally objected to being treated as mere yokels or legitimate figures of fun by those less civilised in their behaviour than themselves. Their inborn courtesy was affronted by the free-and-easy manners and customs of the few who appeared to think that country folk had no more sensibilities than wild animals.

The earliest caravan arrived at Worbarrow over fifty years ago and caused a small sensation. Its owners, the three sisters Thompson, drove it from Surrey with a hired horse and parked it in the field by White Rose Cottage.

One of the Rectory gardeners kept a "Nature Diary" in which one entry read "Steam roller first seen at Tyneham", but I have no record of the date.

Apart from the traction engine of the threshing outfit, steam engines were rarities indeed at Tyneham and found its roads unkindly when they came.

A rash steam-roller, starting to descend from Lawfordshare Gate, got out of control and, throwing off its driver, left the road and tumbled down the hillside, falling to pieces on the way. The roller itself broke loose, careering through a hedge and coming to a standstill in Church Furlong.

I have said little of the indoor servants though I treasure many grateful and affectionate memories of their kindness. I call them "servants" as they would have called themselves, disliking ugly and quibbling euphemisms such as "helps" or "indoor staff", and believing that I could not honour them more than by giving them that fine, proud title which they shared with emperors and popes. For those were days before domestic service was "degrading", and servants thought no shame of following their age-old calling with its honoured traditions. Our footmen did not stay with us long, as a rule, coming from houses where they had worked as pantry boys or pages and passing on to better places after a year or two of training. Sometimes the younger ones were new to service, showing their inexperience by such innocent and engaging slips as knocking on a sitting-room door before they entered. One of her little pages delighted my old grandmother by knocking on her brougham door and addressing her as "Your ladyship".

Our schoolroom meals were served at the square "cat table" in the dining-room by a succession of these cheerful, gawky lads.

The butlers we, as children, had little to do with and we regarded them from a respectful distance as we did the cooks.

A dear friend of our youth was Maggie Drew, a kitchenmaid who shared our love of animals and helped us to prepare our pussies for the Cat and Poultry Shows at Corfe on Boxing Day. The cats, protesting to high heaven, set off in the little waggon before dawn in company with my elder sister's entries in the poultry classes. The competition was not great but we were just as proud of the awards as if they had been gained at the Crystal Palace.

Another very old friend was Isabella Summers, a Winfrith girl who came to us as housemaid and remained for many years. When she had retired and lived in Dorchester she often came back to fill a gap or give us extra help with parlour work at busy times until within a very few years of her death at a good old age. She ran the pantry most efficiently and did far more in far less time than butler and footman put together. Strictly methodical, she could not bear the least departure from routine. An unexpected guest arriving just before a meal would set her in a flutter, "upsetting her corners", as she called it, on the ready laid table. We were all much attached to her, and my father, who pretended to be exasperated by her meticulous ways, was always pleased to see her on her periodical returns. She dressed in the plainest fashion, with prim hats and bonnets, ground-length skirts and square-toed, elastic-sided boots, but made light work of the rough hill walk to Kimmeridge on her frequent visits to her old friend, Mrs. Boyd. The incongruous little figure in its sombre black, holding a large umbrella against wind or sun, tripped lightly over the miles of grassy way, undaunted by the distance or the weather.

Our fondness for her was returned and she shared our love of Tyneham, so that her room in Dorchester was crammed with souvenirs and photographs of house and family.

Of my mother's maids dear Ada Newman (afterwards Mrs. Dell) holds foremost place in my remembrance. She came to us as nursery maid and, when the nursery was no longer needed, stayed on as lady's maid. She still, at eighty years old, remains a trusted and beloved friend. Her home was a farmhouse on the Breamore Estate and she was one of a family of eleven whose names I still remember : Harry and Carrie, Fred and Ted, Lotty and Letty, Frank and Bert, Edith, Ella and Ada. Ada, like all her sisters, was charming in appearance with soft bright hair, blue eyes and rosy cheeks. She looked and was as good as gold. We loved her singing and demanded, over and over again, "The Golden Wedding", "Lazily, Drowsily", "Two Little Girls in Blue", "Father, dear father, come home with me now", "Sophie, go back to your uncle" and "Pop goes the Weasel".

Ada was an avid reader, always endeavouring to improve her mind and, when she set her heart on learning French, I spent many hours in the Cocoanut Room when lessons were over, imparting to her my small stock of the language.

Another lady's maid who lived with us for many years after Ada's marriage was Sophie McLellan, a gentle young Scotswoman of unusual type, in looks the opposite of Ada. Hers was that rarity, a perfectly heart-shaped face, with great, dark, slightly slanted eyes, so wide apart as to give her a calm, remote expression, like that of some noble, meditative bird.

She was a clever dressmaker and always ready to employ her skill in the cause of our theatrical ventures. I think it was she who once complained of our plebeian name. In the larger country houses which she visited with my mother the autocrats of stewards' and housekeepers' rooms ordained that valets and maids be known by their employers' names and served at meals according to their rank. Poor Sophie felt humiliated by her low position at the table and being addressed as "Mrs. Bond", while titles and patrician names resounded in her ears.

On looking back through this discursive record of my memories I find that, in speaking of my mother, I may have given a false impression of her as a stern and unfeeling parent. She was, on the contrary, a most devoted mother, putting her childrens' happiness and welfare above everything else. She took great trouble and was ready for any sacrifice in the cause of our education and was continually trying to interest us in world affairs. I think we learned far more from listening to our elders' conversation than from any other source. It certainly encouraged us to follow up the many subjects we heard talked about at meals or on our walks and added to our stock of general knowledge. My mother had a strong dislike for "personal" topics and would steer the conversation away from them towards subjects of more general interest.

Her views on education, though now long out-dated, must then have been ahead of her time.

When we were very young she bought us kindergarten outfits and taught us how to use them. Skilled with her fingers and with a gift for drawing and script she did her best to make us handy too. I can remember doing fascinating things with squares and strips of coloured paper and having a course of lessons in the Swanage straw work, now a lost art and industry. Even the boys were made to design and work their samplers.

She made big scrap-books out of brightly coloured and glazed calico, stitching them neatly with contrasting thread and, on rainy days, helped us to cut out pictures from the Christmas numbers to decorate the pages. When finished the books were sent to childrens' hospitals.

She read aloud to us, mostly from Scott or Dickens or Kingsley, and I remember one whole thrilling winter of "Lorna Doone". We were brought up on the Victorian nursery classics and, if our minds were warped and blighted by" The Fairchild Family", we were happily unaware of it. Maria Edgeworths' moral stories, "Ministering Children", "Alice", "Uncle Remus", "The Schönberg-Cotta Family", the "Daisy" and "Leila" series, "Masterman Ready", "Swiss Family Robinson" and "Little Women" were well-tried favourites, with Charlotte Yonge's books and "The Wide, Wide World". We loved the Andrew Lang collection of old fairy tales, in volumes bound in all the colours of the rainbow, and knew the whole of Henty, Ballantyne and Manville Fenn by heart. "Black Beauty" was read over and over again and so were Seton Thompson's books and Long's delightful stories of American birds and beasts.

My mother had been Hallé's pupil in her youth and was a pianist of taste besides performing competently on the harp and organ. Her piano playing, as a child of eleven, so delighted the Maharajah Dhuleep Singh that he presented her with a magnificent doll and a pearl and enamel pendant which she treasured to the end of her life. She had a small but true and charming singing voice and her songs are still recalled with pleasure by some who heard her sixty years and more ago.

To poetry she was deaf, except to "Paradise Lost", and so we had to find the poets for ourselves as we grew up.

Belonging to a family of eleven children, six of whom were boys, she had early learned to take hard knocks without complaint and to understand the masculine point of view. She had no sympathy with whining or too easy tears.

To the end of her life she kept her youthful outlook with a special understanding of shy and awkward boys. They took to her instinctively and she showed infinite patience with their troubles, grudging no time spent listening to their problems. The secret of her wonderful success with them may well have lain in the fact that she always sought and found the best in everyone who crossed her path. She could not bear detraction and practised what she taught :—that if no good could be said of an individual it was better to keep silence.

When she died a cousin who had known her well for nearly seventy years declared that she had never heard my mother say an unkind thing or pass on gossip.

She never forgot old servants and a substantial portion of her heavy correspondence consisted of her letters to and on behalf of these valued friends.

My mother's mind was alert to new impressions and she revelled in a fresh experience. She was in her seventies when she drove in a tank at Bovington over banks and ditches and broken ground, enjoying herself thoroughly. She took a daughter out for a trial run in a speed boat when she was over eighty and would have dearly liked to fly when in her nineties.

I think of her as an intrepid traveller eager to see the world, an eagerness which, for the most part, force of circumstances kept unsatisfied, though in imagination she inhabited far outposts of the Empire with the sons whom she had sent out in its service. No thought of distance or of hardship daunted her and she would willingly have plunged into the unknown, with zest and keen anticipation of enjoyment, at any period of her life. She did achieve long visits to Malta and to Omdurman, to see sons serving in those places, and went on a cruise to the Norwegian fiords at the age of eighty-six.

She set great store by courage and self-control and I never saw her lose her head in an emergency or heard her raise her voice in argument or anger.

She could not be put off with second-bests and refused to tolerate slipshod, careless, disrespectful ways. She was a pattern of good manners which she regarded as the necessary oil to make the wheels of life run smoothly. Her quiet and dignity of bearing marked her as the daughter of a lengthy line of Yorkshire gentlefolk and the inheritor of their best qualities, including an unbending sense of duty. Like all her kind she took it as a matter of course that her beloved sons should serve their country at the ends of the earth rather than occupy more lucrative positions nearer home.

I know she was not naturally patient and that she must have gone through bitter struggles before she disciplined herself into the calm of self-possession which was her constant characteristic. For one so full of energy the wearisome restrictions of her latter days, when sight and memory and physical powers were failing, must needs have been a heavy burden. She never complained or showed impatience, remaining gentle, kind and courteous to the end. Those who attended her through those last months were won by her gracious manner and ready gratitude for any little act of service. In this she followed in the footsteps of her mother who, crippled by arthritis for over twenty years, refused to be regarded as an object of compassion and maintained a lively interest in the world around her. My grandmother's excellent memory and hearing never failed her, she read small print without the help of spectacles and could tackle the toughest steak with her own sound teeth to within a few weeks of her death at the age of ninety-two. The mantle of these two women fell upon my brothers who bore protracted suffering with high-hearted gallantry.

My father had inherited his father's fine physique and must have been outstandingly good-looking in his youth. He was a noticeable figure to the end, six feet in height, broad-shouldered and well-made, holding himself erect and looking the person he spoke to straight in the face. He was physically strong, a lifter of heavy weights and able to endure great strain and fatigue.

He hated cruelty and was as gentle with young birds and beasts as he was with babies and small children, for whom, and the babies in particular, he had a special fondness. He was the best of company for children and had an inexhaustible fund of stories, rhymes and sayings, appropriate to all manner of occasions.

His holidays from Temple Grove and Eton had been spent at Tyneham and at South Petherton, his fathers' cure, hunting and shooting with the farmers' sons, learning to love all sides of country life and to notice details of it with an inescapable eye.

He loved to be in company and would, I suppose, in the language of these days be called a very good mixer. He liked to talk to us about his father's drives from South Petherton, whose vicar he (my grandfather) was throughout the whole of his ministry. In the years before his marriage at the age of forty-six my grandfather would often set out on a Sunday, after the evening service, and drive his gig to Tyneham, with single horse or tandem, a forty-five mile journey over indifferently metalled roads. Arriving in the early hours he would feed his horse and rub it down before composing himself on a bale of hay to sleep until the household was astir.

Once, when he took a new dog back with him from Tyneham and loosed it on arrival, it ran into the Vicarage kitchen, where the housekeeper mistook it for a stray and flapped a cloth to drive it out. The dog can never have stopped running until it was back at Tyneham, where it reappeared a few hours later.

My grandfather was anything but self-indulgent. He studied and wrote his sermons and correspondence seated on a narrow coffin-stool and never gave in to the "modern" habit of breakfast. A piece of toast sufficed him until early dinner.

In his early days at Petherton he and his faithful servant, Thomas Cooper, lived in the then unfurnished vicarage, with only the barest of necessities.

It was Thomas who remarked to his master, after they had spent a night at a neighbouring country house : "You gentlemen would never sleep a wink if you knew what was going on downstairs". He went on to describe how he had left the other servants drinking in the hall, the night before, and had found his way up to the mens' rooms, climbing into the nearest bed as no quarters had been assigned him. After some hours the coachman came to claim his bed and kicked the intruder out. Thomas decided thereupon to finish out the night by the kitchen fire and, on his way downstairs, met two of the footmen coming up on hands and knees, too drunk to see him though he carried a lighted candle. This must have been a hundred and thirty years ago.

My grandfather was twenty-six years older than his wife, whom he had christened as an infant. Their only daughter, Edith, died suddenly and tragically at Tyneham at the age of ten and her father's hair turned white in the night of her death.

He twice fought through a smallpox epidemic in his parish with the utmost courage and devotion and his two sons never forgot the tales he told them of the horror of those times. The brothers set their faces rigidly against the granting of exemptions from vaccination when it became compulsory and steadily refused, as magistrates, to sign exemption orders, telling the parents to apply to some other justice of the peace, as they would not have the danger to the children on their consciences. When I was a child a face made hideous by the marks of smallpox was still a common sight.

AND so, at the end of these rambling reminiscences, I come back to the men and women whom I knew at Tyneham, to whom and to whose friendship I have owed so great a measure of my happiness. Contemporary writers give so many false impressions of the rural dweller in the days before the war and I would give much to know that I have helped to prove that at least in one small area they were neither pitiable objects nor rude, brainless clods.

There probably is, or perhaps it would be wiser to say was, no creature in the world more obstinate and stubborn than the Dorset worker on the land.

He had a deep distrust of innovations and, where his own vocation was concerned, was justified in keeping to his own inherited and well-tried ways, resisting all suggestions of more up-to-date methods with immovable tenacity. For even the less skilled labourer was a craftsman, whose craft had come to him through many generations of trained specialists, so that his personal mastery of his materials sprang from the knowledge and experience of men whose lives were spent in perfecting the practice of their trade.

The secrets of the craft were handed on from father to son, the children watching how the work was done as soon as their short legs were strong enough to follow 'Dad' into the woods or fields.

The thatcher's son became a thatcher, the ditcher's son a ditcher, with all the lore of thatching or of ditching in their blood and at their finger-tips.

To take one instance, it is only necessary to compare the old style of hedging with the new in order to perceive the difference between the craftsman's and the untrained tyro's work, though there are still a few fine hedgers practising up and down the county, once so famous for its fencing. Apart from copsing in the winter, woodmen were kept busy through the year, fencing and mending gaps, keeping the hedge-row ditches clean and clearing "bunnies" carrying surface water under paths and rides.

Plashing or plushing hedges was an art not easily learned and called for a true eye and a skilful hand. A well-laid hedge became a thing of beauty taking its right place in the landscape's pattern. No gashed, tormented spikes stood out from the even outline of the fence, so cunningly interwoven that it made a strong unbreakable barrier for the cattle.

It was a pleasure to watch the hedger choose his upright growths and snick them, almost casually, with his unerring blade, twisting them down into the structure of the fence and pinning them in place with

sharpened gads. Where growth was thin the horizontal lay was re-in-
forced by wreath or writh from the copsing, artfully woven in without
apparent join.

At the end of the task, remaining fence material was sorted out and
laid in separate heaps, "scroff" to be burnt up on the spot, good
hedging stuff to go to the next job, and "fackets" for the fire at home.
The hedger took his "nitch" of firewood home with him at the end of
the day.

Part of his business was to choose good saplings here and there
along the fence and spare them to make hedgerow timber. It seems
that this most excellent custom has gone out of favour and that Dorset's
rich inheritance of field grown timber is not now replaced. The loss, in
shelter for cattle and for insect eating birds, in home-grown hardwood,
influence on climate and in beauty is impossible to assess.

The hedger's craft was only one of the many specialised industries
which, taken together, formed the close-knit corporation of the country
workers.

A salient characteristic of the rural dweller of my youth was his
strong individuality. It is impossible to think of him as a mere unit in a
class or "occupational group". Each of those Purbeck men and women
stands out clearly in my memory as a positive personality with his or
her remembered idiosyncracies, and this holds good of every walk of
life. Such people could not be fitted into a mould or form a tidy pattern
for the theorist or statistician. They showed no wish to be conformed
to any mediocre standard in speech or dress or style of living, and the
happy consequence was a variety of character and behaviour adding
colour to the texture of our country life.

Then, as now, what was stated in the press was largely taken "for
Gospel", but newspapers were few and far between and there was
ample time for thinking over and sifting what was read. Each individual
chewed his problems for himself uninfluenced by catch-words or by
mass suggestion and, having arrived at his conclusions, held them
doggedly.

Many farm workers were inarticulate with strangers and kept their
wise reflections to themselves. It needed long acquaintanceship and
mutual trust to bring their real convictions to the light. Political
candidates and canvassers were either baffled by their taciturnity or
humbugged by the appearance of agreement with the views presented
to them. The visitors little knew how long their one-sided discourse
would furnish food for village entertainment.

The Tyneham dwellers naturally resented anything like patronage
or being talked down to by a "furriner" and thoroughly enjoyed a "leg
pull", especially if the leg in question was a pompous one.

A fatuous visitor to Worbarrow once strained the patience of a
group of fishermen by his assumption of superior knowledge. They
listened politely while he told them much that they knew better than
he. At last he pointed to the bay and unctuously enquired: "Does not

this scene remind you of the Lake of Gennesareth?" There was a pause before old Henry Miller said:—"Did 'ee ever zee the Leäke of Ginnynazareth?" The visitor was obliged to answer "No". A quiet "Ah . . ." was the only comment, but it had its effect.

A characteristic instance of the Dorset sense of humour comes to mind, though it cannot be claimed by Tyneham. A village housewife gave a little party, in spite of grumbling on her husband's part, to celebrate some family occasion. As several unexpected guests arrived she whispered to her husband:—"George, do 'ee goo and borrow a vew more cheäirs from neighbours ; us an't got enough". To which her George replied:—"There be plenty of *cheäirs*, missus. 'tis too many *volk*".

The people's speech was pithy and descriptive, free from all commonplace or slang, and was an every day delight to those who lived with them. They spoke when they had something worth the saying and said it in appropriate, telling words, each man or woman's speech being coloured by the speaker's personality. To hear them talk was a real education not only in the age-old lore of country things but also in the proper use of language. Their speech was the dignified, plain English of the Bible, overlaid with dialect and, spoken in the leisurely Dorset voice, it had a poetry and music all its own. Often the ear was captivated by a phrase of sheerest beauty and I never cease regretting that I did not record the sayings while they were fresh in mind. I did not then foresee the vanishing of country speech from the then un-Americanised rural areas.

The study of the Bible was becoming a less universal habit in my youth, but the influence of Scripture was still closely interwoven with the texture of men's daily lives. It still gave dignity to common talk, informed men's judgment and provided them with a philosophy which kept them steadfast in the face of all the chances of mortality.

Sometimes a village tragedy occurred and here and there a man or woman failed to keep faith with the accepted standard. These were the rare exceptions which but emphasized the rule of worthy citizenship.

If I keep silence over these few lapses it is because the stumblers were my neighbours and I am so outmoded as to recoil from a betrayal of their memories.

Perhaps there were scandals in my family, too. I never heard of any but if I had, I still would hold with Sir Alfred Noyes that it is fatuous to believe that filial piety, in saying nought derogatory of a father, deprives a writer's record of authenticity.

The truth remains that the vast majority of agricultural workers of my day were of sterling soundness, worthy of honour for the part they played in England's life.

The land was served by them and by its owners with single-hearted devotion. They put its claims above their own convenience and generously spent their strength and substance in its exacting thraldom.

To men with the inbred consciousness that human life depends upon the soil there could not be any question of downing tools or leaving beasts untended at the striking of a clock.

The agricultural labourer's lot has greatly changed within my memory and I rejoice that life for him and his has lost so many of its hardships. For those who have always longed to see him better rewarded for his toil and able to enjoy a greater freedom it is good indeed to know that he has a larger share of comfort and security. Whether his happiness and contentment have increased is an open question. Do all the temporal improvements in his lot outweigh the eternal values, the pride in work well done, the deep integrity of the worker as I knew and honoured him in pre-war days?

Perhaps the tide may turn again and disregard for much that went to the nation's making will give way to a grateful recognition of the stock whence we are sprung.

No tree can stand or flourish without roots. So many people that I know appear to lack the steadying influence of a close and sympathetic contact with the past. To my mind it is good to know whence we have come and something of the men and women who have made us what we are, to whom we owe it to maintain the traditions of our race.

My family has farmed its lands in Purbeck for five hundred years. Some few of its members have achieved distinction in the larger world, but I am not concerned with "praising famous men". My heart's content is with the lengthy line of ordinary, unassuming men and women of my name without memorial in history who asked no better than to serve their God, their King and country and their poorer neighbours, in the state to which they had been called, without reward or recognition.

These and the thousands like them scattered over England were, to my way of thinking, the real builders of their country's greatness, neither by force of arms nor by industrial success but by devoted service to the land and by the soundness of their lives. Their "privilege" was to serve, a privilege both a burden and an honour. This they believed to be the obligation of their heritage, their humble part in life, and the great majority fulfilled it to their best ability according to their lights.

As has been said of John and Mary Evelyn:—"Perhaps they were greater than the great. Perhaps by their ceaseless endeavour, their purity of motive, their almost instinctive resolve never to abase their standard, their sustained effort to turn the passing hour to good account and their constant preoccupation to help others, they may have set in motion those little currents of influence hidden from the eyes of men, yet reaching further than mortal man can grasp."*

And H. J. Massingham, that doughty champion of the countryman, has said that the "real, fundamental division of our times . . . is not between political parties nor between conflicting ideologies nor even between nations . . . The real division is between rival philosophies of

* Arthur Ponsonby

life. The one believes in exploiting natural resources, the other in conserving them ; the one in centralised control, the other in regional self-government ; the one in conquering and the other in co-operating with nature, the one in chemical and inorganic methods imitated from those of the urban factory and the other in biological and organic ones derived from the observation of nature as a whole ; the one in man as a responsible agent with freewill to choose between the good and the bad ; the other [in man] as a unit of production directed from above by an élite of technologists and bureaucrats ; the one in the divine creation both of man and nature, and the other in man as self-sufficient in himself, with nature merely as the means for extracting wealth for himself. The one philosophy is dominant and possesses all the power but the other is in possession of the *truth*".

The English squires are riding to the sea. Most of them have already passed from sight and, such is the power of town-dictated mass opinion, their going is regarded with indifference if not with satisfaction and with ill-informed abuse. Perhaps there is no place left for them in a slick and glossy world where getting on and getting rich are the main objectives and where values must be reckoned by a monetary standard. The land they loved, for which they sacrificed so much, the land to which they and their followers gave such loyal service, knows them no more. It is, for the most part, left to the tender mercies of the opportunist, whose only use for it is to strip and exhaust it for the sake of quick returns.

It cannot be that the centuries of faithful care and toil have been in vain. A day must surely come, and may it come before it is too late, when saner principles will reassert themselves and the wise and self-denying service of our forefathers will have its recognition.

Without these cannot a city be inhabited:
And they shall not dwell where they will, nor go up and down:
They shall not be sought for in publick counsel,
Nor sit high in the congregation:
They shall not sit on the judge's seat,
Nor understand the sentence of judgment:
They cannot declare justice and judgment,
And they shall not be found where parables are spoken,
But they will maintain the state of the world,
And all their desire is in the work of their craft".*

May they rest in peace

Dorchester.
Feast of S. Benedict, 1955

* Ecclesiasticus 38

135